Balancing Act—
Debt, Deficits, and Taxes

Edited by John H. Makin,
Norman J. Ornstein, and
David Zlowe

WITHDRAWN

The AEI Press

Publisher for the American Enterprise Institute
WASHINGTON, D.C.

1990

Acknowledgments

The conference and volume were made possible by generous grants from the Pew Charitable Trusts and the Ford Foundation. We thank them for their continuing support.

The conference on which this book is based took place at the Madison Hotel in Washington, D.C., on January 16, 1990. The editors are grateful to the staffs of the Madison Hotel and the American Enterprise Institute for its success. In particular we would like to thank Isabel Davidov, Don Flick, and Mark Schmitt of AEI. We remember with gratitude the contributions of the late Mark Steinbruck.

JHM, NJO, DAZ

Distributed by arrangement with

UPA, Inc.
4720 Boston Way   3 Henrietta Street
Lanham, Md. 20706   London WC2E 8LU England

Library of Congress Cataloging-in-Publication Data

Balancing act : debt, deficits, and taxes / edited by John H. Makin, Norman J. Ornstein, and David Zlowe.
   p. cm.
  Includes bibliographical references.
  ISBN 0-8447-3740-2
  1. Budget deficits—United States. 2. Debts, External—United States. 3. Fiscal policy—United States. I. Makin, John H. II. Ornstein, Norman J. III. Zlowe, David.
HJ2052.B35   1990
339.5'23'0973—dc20   90-19659
                                                      CIP

AEI Studies 517

Printed in the United States of America

Contents

Contributors

RUDIGER DORNBUSCH has been the Ford International Professor of Economics at Massachusetts Institute of Technology since 1985. At MIT since 1975, he has published numerous articles, books, and textbooks on general economics and international economics. He is the coauthor of two standard texts in economics: *Macroeconomics* (1987, with Stanley Fischer), and *Economics* (1987, with Stanley Fischer and Richard Schmalensee). He is an associate editor of the *Quarterly Journal of Economics* and the *Journal of International Economics*. He is also a research associate at the National Bureau of Economic Research.

BILL GRADISON represents the second congressional district of Ohio in the U.S. House of Representatives, where he serves on both the House Budget Committee and the House Committee on Ways and Means. On Ways and Means he is the ranking Republican member of the Health Subcommittee and also serves on the Social Security Subcommittee. On the Budget Committee he represents the House Republican leader. He is chairman of the House Wednesday Group and chairman of the American Enterprise Institute's Economic Roundtable.

G. WILLIAM HOAGLAND is the minority staff director of the U.S. Senate Committee on the Budget. He has been staff director, deputy staff director, and senior analyst for agriculture and natural resources on the committee. Mr. Hoagland was administrator of the Food and Nutrition Service at the Department of Agriculture and special assistant for food and nutrition policy to the secretary of agriculture. From 1975 to 1981 he worked in the Congressional Budget Office on income security issues, tax policy, and food and nutrition policies. His two most recent publications are "The Distribution of Benefits from the 1982 Federal Crop Program" and "Perceptions and Reality in Nutrition Programs," published by the American Enterprise Institute in *Maintaining the Safety Net*.

JACK F. KEMP is the secretary of housing and urban development, where he is responsible for federally assisted economic development and housing programs. Mr. Kemp represented the thirty-first congressional district of New York in the U.S. House of Representatives from 1970 to 1988. He was chairman of the House Republican Conference for seven years and was a member of the House Appropriations Committee and a ranking member of the Foreign Operations Subcommittee.

LAWRENCE J. KORB is director of the Center for Public Policy Education and senior fellow in the foreign policy studies program at the Brookings Institution. He served as dean of the Graduate School of Public and International Affairs at the University of Pittsburgh. As assistant secretary of defense for manpower, reserve affairs, installations, and logistics from 1981 to 1985, he administered about 70 percent of the defense budget. He is a member of the Council on Foreign Relations, the International Institute of Strategic Studies, and the National Academy of Public Administration. His publications about national defense include *The Joint Chiefs of Staff: The First Twenty-Five Years* and *The Fall and Rise of the Pentagon*.

JOHN H. MAKIN is the director of fiscal policy studies at the American Enterprise Institute. He was the director of the Institute for Economic Research and professor of economics at the University of Washington in Seattle. He has conducted extensive research on international trade and finance, monetary theory and policy, interest rate and exchange rate behavior, and tax and budget policy. His most recent major publication is *Sharing World Leadership? A New Era for America and Japan* coedited with Donald C. Hellmann. Dr. Makin also serves as chairman of the Japan-United States Friendship Commission and the United States-Japan Conference on Cultural and Educational Interchange.

NORMAN J. ORNSTEIN is a resident scholar at the American Enterprise Institute. He is a political contributor to the MacNeil/Lehrer News-Hour and an election analyst for CBS News. His books include *The People, Press and Politics, The American Elections of 1982, The New Congress, Interest Groups, Lobbying and Policymaking*, and *Vital Statistics on Congress*, now in its fourth edition. He was a staff member and staff director from 1976 to 1977 of the Senate Committee to Study the Committee System, which reorganized the Senate.

RUDOLPH G. PENNER has been a senior fellow at the Urban Institute since 1987. He was the director of the Congressional Budget Office from 1983 through 1987 and director of fiscal policy studies and resident scholar at the American Enterprise Institute from 1977 to 1983. He has been the assistant director for economic policy at the Office of Management and Budget, deputy assistant secretary for economic affairs at the Department of Housing and Urban Development, and senior staff economist at the Council of Economic Advisers. He has written many books and articles. His most recent book, cowritten with Alan Abramson, is *Broken Purse Strings*, a study of the congressional budget process.

JAMES M. POTERBA is a professor of economics at Massachusetts Institute of Technology, where he has taught since 1982. He is a research associate at the National Bureau of Economic Research and a fellow of the Econometric Society. Dr. Poterba's current research focuses on the economic effects of taxing corporate capital income, as well as on statistical modeling of stock price movements. He is coauthor of two recent studies, *Manufacturing in America's Future* and *Over-consumption: The Challenge to U.S. Economic Policy*, which examine national saving in the United States.

C. EUGENE STEUERLE is a senior fellow at the Urban Institute and the author of a weekly column for *Tax Notes*. Between 1987 and 1989 he was the deputy assistant secretary of the Treasury for tax analysis. Among his many books and articles about public finance and taxation are *Taxes, Loans and Inflation* and *Who Should Pay for Collecting Taxes? Financing the IRS*. He was the director of finance and taxation projects and a resident fellow at the American Enterprise Institute and a federal executive fellow at the Brookings Institution.

DAVID ZLOWE is a research associate in fiscal policy studies at the American Enterprise Institute. He was a special analyst for the Senate Budget Committee on infrastructure financing. Mr. Zlowe has worked at the Hudson Institute on fiscal policy and budget issues. His books include *Alternative Solutions to Developing-Country Debt Problems* (coedited with Rudiger Dornbusch and John H. Makin). His current research focuses on U.S.-Japan relations and on fiscal policy and budgeting in the United States.

Introduction

David Zlowe

An attempt to envisage the path of fiscal policy during the decade may be considered bold, if not foolhardy. The nature of the fiscal challenges to the United States cannot be known with certainty from week to week, much less from decade to decade.

The exercise can also be useful, however, as the reader will observe. The contributors to this volume focus on specific challenges to the economy and how they will be met. They move beyond the fashionable platitudes of the day into a productive discussion about long-term strategies for our policy makers.

In spite of such perceived economic challenges as high deficits, low productivity, and low saving, the mood of the contributors is fairly upbeat. Our fiscal threats seem to have solutions in the universe of achievable policy. We have the policy tools well at hand—all we lack, it would seem, is the political will to use them. This climate is poles apart from the gloom of a decade ago, when economists and policy makers did not even seem to know what was wrong, much less whether and how these ills could be corrected. In fact, a survey of the news and attitudes from early 1980 about the nation's prospects for the rest of that decade might lend a useful note of caution and insight to the conclusions drawn in this volume about the 1990s.

In the closing days of 1979 the Soviet military moved in force into Afghanistan. During the first week of the new decade, President Carter embargoed grain as a weapon against the Soviet Union. He would later boycott the 1980 Olympic Games in Moscow and begin draft registration. On January 22 the Soviet government exiled from Moscow Nobel laureate Andrei Sakharov. Meanwhile in Iran, the fifty-two embassy hostages were counting their second month of captivity. The *Bulletin of Atomic Scientists* moved the hands of the "doomsday clock," calibrating the likelihood of a nuclear holocaust, from nine minutes before midnight to seven minutes before midnight.[1]

On the domestic scene, the energy crisis continued as citizens recalled President Carter's televised July 15, 1979 "crisis of confidence" speech. The ill-fated Synthetic Fuels Corporation was formed, to be funded by a windfall profits tax on oil companies. Also in early January, President Carter signed the Chrysler bailout plan. While unemployment held at 5.9 percent (then considered to be "full employment," although the unemployment rate has recently been as low as 5.1 percent of the work force), gold soared to $835 per ounce in London. The prime rate was near 15 percent, and heading higher. On January 10 the Federal Reserve announced that the M2 measurement of the money supply had grown by 8.3 percent in 1979. On January 18, however, the Department of Commerce announced that the GNP increased only by 2.3 percent after inflation, and a week later the Labor Department announced that consumer prices had risen by 13.3 percent in 1979. All those extra dollars seemed to be chasing higher prices; all they bought was stagflation.

In the *Brookings Papers on Economic Activity*, editor George L. Perry stated that "the 1970s will be remembered as the most disappointing decade for economic performance since the Great Depression."[2] The chairman of the President's Council of Economic Advisers, Charles L. Schultze, commented that the 1981 budget was "the first time any administration's budget has officially forecast a recession in advance of its actually occurring."[3] In AEI's *Contemporary Economic Problems* from 1979, however, Gottfried Haberler summed up the real problem:

> Easy monetary-fiscal policy to reduce unemployment accelerates inflation, while a tight money-fiscal policy to curb inflation increases unemployment. This policy dilemma has caused a feeling of helplessness and malaise. . . . [T]here is no crisis of capitalism, no malfunctioning of the market economy, but a crisis of government policies. The stagflation dilemma is the predictable consequence of faulty government policies . . . [which include] the exploding propensity to control and regulate the economy.[4]

In Washington, the *National Journal*, a magazine which focuses on the government, entitled its January 19, 1980 cover story, "Can We Govern? The Traumas of the 70s—The Challenges of the 80s."[5] The introduction to the 1980 edition of *The Almanac of American Politics* said,

> As the nation enters the political year of 1980, an unmistakable mood of depression and uncertainty lies across the land. . . . A majority of Americans doubt that government can do anything to solve the country's big problems.[6]

Yet a majority still believed President Carter could govern. A Gallup poll released January 9 showed that 58 percent of respondents approved of Carter's handling of the presidency. Moreover, the poll showed Carter leading Ronald Reagan 63 to 32 percent in the presidential contest.

Prospects did not look good for Ronald Reagan in January 1980. At a Republican presidential candidate debate in Des Moines, Iowa on January 21, the day of the precinct caucuses, candidate John Anderson advocated a 50 cent a gallon tax on gasoline, accompanied by a social security tax cut (he may have been ten years ahead of his time, as some of the following pages suggest). Later that day, George Bush enjoyed the big momentum of his victory over Ronald Reagan in the caucuses. After his "Big Mo" turned into "Slow Mo," however, it took eight years for him to become president.

As the first month of the 1980s drew to a close, all that seemed certain was the dominance of the Pittsburgh Steelers over the Los Angeles Rams in Superbowl XIV (the score was 31–19). The Steelers seemed to be a constant, winning their fourth Superbowl in six years. They were not destined, however, to win the Superbowl again in the 1980s. Even sustained success on the playing field was not carried into the 1980s. In so many ways, the 1980s would look very different from the 1970s.

Given the conditions in January 1980, any pessimistic forecasting for the 1980s can be excused. The political and economic scenes changed dramatically during the decade. Now in 1990, we have seen the atomic scientists turn back their doomsday clock as the Soviet empire has collapsed and nuclear missiles are being dismantled. The late Andrei Sakharov is now seen as a saint by many in the USSR. George Bush sits in the White House enjoying his first term, not having been elected in 1980 or 1984. The economy sustained eight years of growth, with lower interest rates, lower inflation, and lower unemployment. The savings rate has risen again, and the federal budget deficit and merchandise trade deficit are on downward trends as percentages of the gross national product.

Most striking about the following pages is what is *not* said. Talk of a "malaise" is long gone. The contributors do not express concern that the nation and economy cannot be governed, however; they fervently hope that policy makers will choose to govern. There is no longer soaring inflation or unemployment to demand concern and attention. More technical and less glamorous issues can be addressed. They ask, for example, What is the interest rate effect of budget deficits? Should social security's trust fund be on or off the budget? Since we all agree that defense spending is going down, how fast should it decline? What is the long-term consequence of our current savings rate?

While some of these questions should concern policy makers, they are of a nature fundamentally different from, Can we govern? In the 1980s perhaps we needed an ideologue in the White House who could answer that question. In the 1990s the nation seems to want a pragmatist who can address narrower issues. Apparently, then, the issues that used to buffet policy makers have quieted down. That's good. Crises do not produce wise long-term public policy.

The question for the 1990s differs from that of the 1980s. We know we can govern. The question is, What do we want? In his paper, Rudolph Penner shows us how much some of our wants will cost. Rudiger Dornbusch and James Poterba make some suggestions about economic policy priorities, with an insightful international comparison. Eugene Steuerle looks at the options for tax policy in the new decade. The discussion by Rep. Bill Gradison, G. William Hoagland, and Larry Korb shows once again that our wants may well exceed our capacity and willingness to pay. Finally, Jack Kemp, coauthor of the 1981 Kemp-Roth tax cut and now secretary of the Department of Housing and Urban Development, looks back at America's economic performance and forward to a bright future.

Overlooking downtown Washington, D.C., is the Naval Observatory. It houses a telescope that can be aimed at the heavens to look "back" in time millions of years. Whenever I pass it I am reminded that we can look back ten years with infinitely more certainty than we can look forward even one day. For displaying the courage of soothsayers, as well as making valuable observations, the contributors to this volume should be commended.

The contributors were participants in a conference held by the American Enterprise Institute at the Madison Hotel in Washington, D.C., on January 16, 1990.

1
Debt and Deficits in the 1990s

Rudiger Dornbusch and James M. Poterba

This is not the first time in this century that the budget deficit and debt problems have been in the forefront of public discussion. In the 1930s the budget was a major issue; and in the 1950s, when the ratio of debt to income was far higher than today, the Eisenhower administration worked hard to balance the budget and thus avoid a growing public debt.[1] In the current debate, there are three special circumstances: First, although debt debates occur typically in the aftermath of a war, today the discussion takes place after decades of peace. Second, although discussion about prudent limits on deficits typically occurs when the economy is depressed—in the 1930s, for example— the current debate is taking place at full employment, following a decade of prosperity. Third, although debates on debts and deficits normally occur when one or the other, measured as a share of GNP, is unusually high, this is not the case for the debt or the deficit ratio in the United States today.

We briefly summarize here the main findings and conclusions of our study:

- The United States decidedly does not face a public debt crisis. Protracted deficits at full employment do not have precedent in U.S. history, but their size is now moderate enough that no snowballing of public debt lies ahead. These facts do not, however, support complacency.
- Persistent deficits, combined with low private saving, reduce investment and hence worsen the prospects for a rising standard of living. The deficits do not add to investment, but rather subtract from it. Contrary to what some theories, such as the Barro-Ricardo hypothesis, might suggest, they have not brought along an offsetting increase in private saving.
- A portion of investment is now financed by foreign lending. Reliance on foreign saving, though preferable to not investing at all, brings with it two difficulties. First, there is a risk of frictions, especially in regard to foreign direct investment. As foreign investors

1

increasingly acquire U.S. real assets, concerns about sovereignty and dependence, almost entirely imagined, come alive. Although foreign direct investment more likely than not creates good jobs at good wages, it provokes hostile reactions. Second, debt service will ultimately require a swing in our trade balance. The longer we pursue a strategy of borrowing, the larger the adjustment ultimately required to generate the surpluses to service our external balance.

• Correction of the deficits will require measures on both the spending and revenue sides.

• The U.S. debt ratio is nowhere near levels that require actual debt retirement to ensure economic and financial stability. Few would agree today with E. H. Young, who commented in 1915: "National debt is like a toothache; it is best not to have one, but if you have got one it is next best to get rid of it as soon as you can."[2] But that is not to say that the growth of debt should not be limited sharply by a more responsible fiscal policy.

Brief History of Debt and Deficits

The federal deficits of the 1980s are not the largest in U.S. history, and the ratio of government debt to gross national product in 1989 is well below its level in the late 1940s and throughout the 1950s, as figure 1-1 illustrates. Why, then, are recent events labeled an unusual fiscal experiment? The answer is twofold: the 1980s were marked by the largest peacetime deficits in U.S. history; and periods of robust economic expansion are traditionally times for repaying federal debts, not incurring new liabilities.

Trends in Federal Borrowing. The federal debt is the federal government's total liability to private investors. Whenever federal tax receipts fall short of government outlays, the Treasury Department must borrow, typically by selling short-term Treasury bills or longer-term bonds to the public. These bonds and bills add to the federal debt. In some cases, the Treasury borrows from other branches of the federal government, such as Federal Reserve banks and retirement trust funds such as the social security or railroad retirement trust. Debt held by Federal Reserve banks or other federal agencies is excluded in calculating the federal debt, because such debt is both an asset and a liability of the federal government. At the end of 1988, federal debt totaled $2.68 trillion, with $1.85 trillion held by private investors, $589 billion by federal trust funds, and $238 billion by Federal Reserve banks. Only the privately held debt affects capital accumulation and other aspects of economic activity, so it is the focus of our subsequent discussion.

FIGURE 1–1
The U.S. Debt-GNP Ratio, 1918–1988

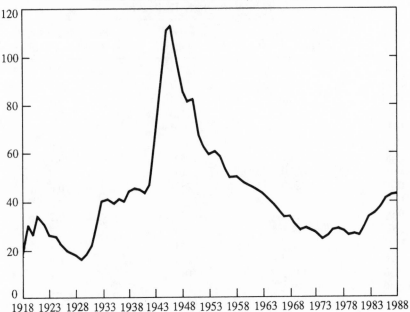

Source: Author.

Table 1–1 shows the evolution of the federal debt over the past two centuries, including its marked growth during the 1980s. In absolute magnitude, the real federal debt is currently larger than at any other time in our nation's history, but not by as much as alarmist calculations focusing on nominal debt stocks would suggest. Although the real value of the government debt is now higher than that of the peak shown in 1945, the difference in real debt stocks is much smaller than the difference in nominal debt. The effects of compound inflation make comparisons based on nominal debt values quite misleading.

Even comparing real debt levels provides an incomplete guide to debt burdens, however, since the U.S. economy is much larger today than in 1945. The second column of table 1–1 shows that, measured as a share of gross national product, the federal debt in 1988 was only one-third as large as that in 1945. The current ratio (.38) is substantially below those of the late 1940s and the 1950s. Nevertheless, the debt ratio has increased by seventeen percentage points since 1980, a far larger increase than in any other peacetime decade.

TABLE 1–1
U.S. PUBLIC DEBT, 1790–1988

	Real Debt[a] ($billions, 1988)	Debt/GNP (percentage)	Real Debt Per Capita[b] ($thousands, 1988)
1790	1.6	31.0	0.4
1800	1.1	18.0	0.2
1810	0.8	8.0	0.1
1820	1.6	11.0	0.2
1830	1.1	4.0	0.1
1840	0.0	0.0	0.0
1850	1.3	3.0	0.1
1860	1.1	1.0	0.0
1870	24.1	25.0	0.6
1880	24.1	13.0	0.5
1890	11.4	5.0	0.2
1900	17.0	5.0	0.2
1910	12.5	3.0	0.1
1920	155.1	27.0	1.5
1930	134.2	16.2	1.1
1940	379.1	41.0	2.9
1945	1,593.1	106.6	11.4
1950	999.5	68.9	6.6
1955	919.4	50.3	5.6
1960	825.3	40.3	4.6
1965	797.3	31.3	4.1
1970	661.5	22.6	3.2
1975	706.2	21.9	3.3
1980	854.0	22.6	3.7
1981	885.5	22.8	3.8
1982	1,028.6	26.8	4.4
1983	1,196.3	30.0	5.1
1984	1,371.6	32.1	5.8
1985	1,557.4	35.3	6.5
1986	1,716.1	37.9	7.1
1987	1,814.4	38.6	7.4
1988	1,852.8	38.0	7.5

a. Real value of debt on December 31.
b. Ratio of column 1 to the total population.
SOURCE: Entries in the first two columns are drawn from Robert J. Barro, *Macroeconomics* (New York: Wiley, 1988), p. 378, updated using various issues of the Federal Reserve Bulletin and converted to 1988 dollars. Population data were drawn from *Historical Statistics of the United States, Colonial Times to 1970* (Washington, D.C.: U.S. Government Printing Office, 1975), with updates from *Current Population Reports*.

The final column in table 1–1 reports real debt per capita. An alternative measure of real debt burdens scaled by the size of the economy, it is the easiest measure to interpret. The net effect of deficit policies was equivalent to each family of four borrowing over $15,000. Yet few households seem to perceive the liabilities the federal government has incurred on their behalf.

The rapid growth in government debt during the 1980s is particularly unusual in light of the robust performance of the U.S. economy since 1983. At the beginning of the 1980s, estimates of the relationship between debt accumulation and economic conditions from previous U.S. experience[3] suggested that a one percentage point reduction in unemployment rate reduced the annual rate of real debt growth by .028 percent. These estimates would have predicted a growth in real debt of 31 percent from 1983 to 1988, when in fact real debt increased by 80 percent. The departure from history is even clearer in 1987 and 1988, when falling unemployment rates would have predicted only a 1.7 percent growth of real debt, but the actual pattern was an 8 percent real increase. The unique character of the 1980s' deficits is therefore the departure from the past patterns of debt accumulation.

Doomsayers often argue that the debt accumulation of the 1980s is also unusual because it has been financed by foreigners. When foreign investors hold U.S. Treasury bonds, the debt is no longer an "inside" liability of the U.S. economy, a debt we owe to ourselves. While foreigners have become important suppliers of capital to the U.S. economy during the past decade, and while the deficit is partly responsible for this phenomenon, direct concern about foreign ownership of government debt is misplaced.

Table 1–2 shows the ownership pattern of Treasury debt. Most

TABLE 1–2

PERCENTAGE OWNERSHIP OF U.S. GOVERNMENT DEBT, 1970–1988

Investor Class	December 1970	December 1980	December 1988
Commercial banks	27.2	18.8	11.2
Insurance companies	3.2	3.3	7.4
State and local governments	12.1	12.8	15.8
U.S. individuals	35.3	21.0	10.1
Foreign investors	9.0	20.7	18.3
Nonfinancial corporations	3.2	4.2	4.7
Others	10.0	19.3	32.5

SOURCE: Federal Reserve Bulletin, January 1976, January 1983, July 1989.

federal debt is held by U.S. citizens. Just over 10 percent of the debt is held directly by individual investors, but nearly two-thirds is held indirectly—through pension funds, banks, or insurance companies in which individuals own stock. Although foreign investors currently hold 18 percent of federal debt, table 1–2 shows that the share of debt held by foreigners has not increased during the 1980s—it was in fact larger in 1980 than in 1989.

Another popular claim among those who profess concern with current debt levels is that increased federal borrowing during the past decade is troublesome because of the increase in private borrowing during the same period. An increasingly indebted economy may be more volatile in response to external shocks, such as those propagated across sectors by bankruptcies at highly leveraged firms or by credit-laden households. Figure 1–2 shows the ratio of net debt outstanding—the sum of private, corporate, and government borrowing—as a share of GNP for the past three decades. Private debt has increased from an average of roughly 1.3 times GNP during the 1960s and 1970s to nearly 1.8 times GNP today. Increased borrowing by corporations has been particularly noteworthy, with many firms issuing debt to repurchase equity.

FIGURE 1–2

PRIVATE AND PUBLIC DEBT AS A PERCENTAGE OF GNP, 1960–1990

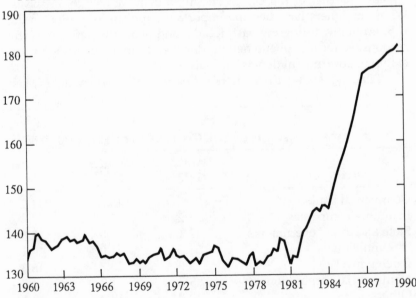

SOURCE: Author.

6

Whether the currently elevated level of private debt makes public debt particularly burdensome is an open question, depending critically on the reason for the recent growth in private borrowing. At least part of the increase is due to financial innovation, changes which have reduced the real costs of financial distress. Two examples of such changes are actively traded junk bonds, in which the borrowers' risk is diversified much as that of equity holders in previous periods, and "strip financing," in which the same investors provide both debt and equity finance, thereby avoiding traditional negotiation costs between claimants if the firm fails. For households, the growth of home equity credit lines represents a new form of secured borrowing, and the risks of such debt from the lender's perspective may be smaller than that on personal loans of previous eras.

Trends in Federal Deficits. The federal deficit is the amount by which federal outlays exceed federal receipts. This simple measure fails to capture many important dimensions of fiscal policy, however, and is therefore best examined with several modified deficit measures.[4]

The first modification to the reported deficit corrects for business cycle variation in federal fiscal conditions. Federal tax receipts rise in periods of strong economic expansion and contract during slack times. Federal outlays, however, expand during periods of weak economic activity, as payouts for various transfer programs, social security benefits, and other programs increase. The full employment deficit, which describes the net federal deficit or surplus if current tax and spending programs remained in force but the economy were at full employment, corrects reported deficit statistics for cyclical changes by standardizing revenues and outlays to a single point in the business cycle. One could analogously adjust the federal debt to reflect the sequence of economic events that prevailed during its accumulation. A large federal debt after a long recession would translate into a smaller cyclically adjusted debt than a similar debt after a long expansion.

A second important problem is that neither the conventional deficit nor the "full employment deficit" correctly accounts for the effects of inflation on the government's fiscal position. Most federal debts are specified in nominal terms. Inflation therefore improves the government's real balance sheet by reducing the value of outstanding debt as well as the monetary base, another government liability. The inflation-adjusted deficit adds a measure of the inflationary gain on nominal government liabilities to the conventional deficit measure. The inflation-adjusted deficit is defined as the reported deficit less the inflation rate within a year times the sum of government bonds and the monetary base at the end of the previous year. The adjustment is analogous to measuring the federal debt at market value, rather than simply as the cumulation of the book value of prior debt issues.

Table 1–3 presents summary statistics on the deficit (or surplus) and the two adjusted measures for the postwar period as reported in the National Income and Product Accounts (NIPA). These data differ from the deficit or surplus numbers used in congressional budgetary discussions in that they exclude asset purchases or sales, which have on balance reduced congressional measures of the deficit during the 1980s.

The last column of data in table 1–4 reports the federal deficit or surplus after adjustment for both inflation and cyclical effects. While still an imperfect measure of government fiscal policy for reasons discussed below, this provides the single most informative measure of deficit policy. This data series also demonstrates the unusual nature of the peacetime deficits in the mid-1980s.

Increased government outlays accounted for a significant part of the deficit expansion between the 1970s and early 1980s, while reduced taxes were responsible for much of the 1981–1984 increase. To provide more detail on the source of both spending and revenue fluctuations, table 1–4 disaggregates the two sides of the federal deficit into major tax and expenditure categories.

The increase in expenditures between the 1970s and 1980s can be traced primarily to an increase in transfers, sharp growth in real interest payments due to both increased federal borrowing and higher real interest rates, and some expansion of federal military spending. Transfers to states and localities as well as nondefense expenditures actually declined between the 1970s and the mid-1980s. With respect to tax collections, table 1–5 shows a decline in corporate tax revenues as a share of GNP during this period. This reflects lower corporate profit rates during the 1980s as well as the corporate tax reductions in the Economic Recovery Tax Act of 1981. Personal income tax collections also dipped in the early 1980s, reflecting the 25 percent reductions in marginal tax rates in the 1981 tax reform.

Unresolved Measurement Issues in Federal Fiscal Policy. Depending on the purpose, different measures may provide more or less reliable guides to government activity. This section addresses how these issues affect the deficit calculus.

Capital budgeting. Current federal accounting practice enters the full amount of any purchase into government spending, regardless of whether the purchase is durable. This procedure does not reflect

TABLE 1–3
FEDERAL OUTLAYS, RECEIPTS, AND DEFICITS-SURPLUSES AS A PERCENTAGE OF GNP, 1950–1988

	Outlays	Receipts	Reported Deficit-Surplus	Business cycle	Inflation	Cycle and inflation
1950	14.3	17.5	3.2	NA	7.1	NA
1951	17.4	19.4	2.0	NA	4.0	NA
1952	20.3	19.3	−1.1	NA	0.8	NA
1953	20.9	18.9	−1.9	NA	−2.2	NA
1954	18.9	17.2	−1.6	NA	0.2	NA
1955	16.9	18.0	1.1	0.8	3.1	2.9
1956	16.9	18.3	1.4	1.3	3.7	3.7
1957	17.8	18.3	0.5	0.6	2.0	2.1
1958	19.6	17.4	−2.3	−1.0	−1.2	0.0
1959	18.5	18.3	−0.2	−0.2	0.9	1.0
1960	18.2	18.8	0.6	0.9	1.2	1.6
1961	19.3	18.5	−0.7	0.0	−0.1	0.6
1962	19.4	18.7	−0.7	−0.7	0.4	0.4
1963	19.0	19.0	0.0	0.0	0.6	0.5
1964	18.4	17.9	−0.5	−1.0	0.1	−0.4
1965	17.8	17.8	0.1	−1.0	1.2	0.2
1966	18.8	18.6	−0.2	−1.9	1.2	−0.4
1967	20.3	18.7	−1.6	−3.0	−0.8	−2.2
1968	20.5	19.8	−0.7	−2.3	1.1	−0.5
1969	19.8	20.7	0.9	−0.4	2.5	1.2
1970	20.5	19.2	−1.2	−1.1	0.2	0.4
1971	20.4	18.4	−2.0	−1.5	−0.3	0.1
1972	20.5	19.1	−1.4	−1.3	−0.2	−0.1
1973	19.8	19.4	−0.4	−1.0	1.7	1.1
1974	20.7	20.0	−0.8	−0.6	1.6	1.8
1975	22.8	18.5	−4.3	−2.8	−2.4	−0.9
1976	22.1	19.1	−3.0	−2.1	−1.5	−0.7
1977	21.6	19.3	−2.3	−2.1	−0.5	−0.4
1978	20.9	19.6	−1.3	−2.0	0.8	0.1
1979	20.8	20.1	−0.3	−1.4	1.6	0.8
1980	22.5	20.3	−2.2	−2.2	0.2	0.3
1981	23.0	20.9	−2.1	−1.8	0.1	0.4
1982	24.7	20.1	−4.6	−2.7	−3.2	−1.3
1983	24.5	19.4	−5.2	−3.5	−4.1	−2.4

Deficit-Surplus Adjusted for: (column headings: Business cycle, Inflation, Cycle and inflation)

(Table continues on next page.)

TABLE 1–3 *(continued)*

	Outlays	Receipts	Reported Deficit-Surplus	Deficit-Surplus Adjusted for:		
				Business cycle	Inflation	Cycle and inflation
1984	23.7	19.2	−4.5	−4.1	−3.4	−3.0
1985	24.5	19.6	−4.9	−4.8	−3.9	−3.8
1986	24.5	19.6	−4.9	−4.9	−3.9	−3.9
1987	23.7	20.1	−3.6	−3.9	−2.3	−2.7
1988	22.9	19.9	−3.0	−3.8	−1.4	−2.1
1950–59	18.2	18.3	0.1	NA	1.8	NA
1960–69	19.2	18.9	−0.3	−0.9	0.8	0.1
1970–79	21.0	19.3	−1.7	−1.6	0.1	0.2
1980–88	23.8	19.9	−3.9	−3.5	−2.4	−2.0

NOTE: The NIPA (see source note below) deficit differs from the conventionally reported federal deficit because it is calculated on an income basis, that is, excludes asset purchases or sales. Since asset sales were used systematically throughout the 1980s to reduce the measured federal deficit, the NIPA deficit is somewhat larger.

SOURCE: Each entry is the corresponding entry from table 1–2 divided by gross national product from the National Income and Product Accounts (NIPA).

the fact that capital goods provide services for many periods. Many states and most other countries maintain a separate budgetary account for capital outlays and include only capital depreciation, not outlays, in their current budget. If the United States followed such a budgeting strategy, the growth in the federal deficit between the 1970s and 1980s would look even larger than measures in table 1–3 suggest.

Table 1–5 reports gross federal investment in nondefense capital as well as depreciation on the existing capital stock. Defense capital is excluded because its durability is difficult to measure (and sometimes random!) and because substantial policy attention is currently devoted to the "infrastructure crisis." Net federal investment has declined by nearly 40 percent since the late 1970s. While the absolute level of federal capital outlays increased from the early to late 1970s, that pattern was reversed in the 1980s. The substantial capital investments of the 1960s, for example in the interstate highway system, raised depreciation during the 1980s, while federal investment declined. This led to a sharp fall in net investment from $16.1 billion (1982 dollars) in 1975–1979 to $9.8 billion in fiscal 1989.

Just as the current accounting practice books all outlays immedi-

TABLE 1-4
Composition of Federal Receipts and Outlays as a Percentage of GNP, 1950–1988

	1950s	1960s	1970s	1980–88	1980–84	1985	1986	1987	1988
Revenues									
Personal taxes	8.0	8.4	8.6	8.9	9.1	8.6	8.5	9.0	8.5
Corporate taxes	5.0	3.8	2.7	1.6	1.6	1.5	1.6	1.8	1.9
FRB revenues	0.1	0.2	0.3	0.4	0.4	0.4	0.4	0.4	0.4
Customs and excise	2.7	2.3	1.5	1.4	1.5	1.4	1.2	1.2	1.2
Social insurance tax	2.5	4.2	6.1	7.5	7.5	7.7	7.9	7.8	8.0
Expenditures									
Military	10.1	8.4	5.8	6.1	6.2	6.5	6.6	6.5	6.1
Nondefense goods and services	1.7	2.2	2.3	2.2	2.0	2.4	2.1	1.9	1.7
Transfers to states and localities	0.9	1.7	3.1	2.6	2.5	2.5	2.5	2.3	2.3
Net interest	1.3	1.2	1.4	2.8	3.1	3.2	3.2	3.1	3.1
Transfers to persons	3.8	4.9	7.9	9.5	9.4	9.5	9.5	9.2	9.0

Source: National Income and Product Accounts, table 3.1.

11

TABLE 1–5

FEDERAL NONDEFENSE CAPITAL INVESTMENT, 1970–1989

(BILLIONS OF 1982 DOLLARS)

	Gross Investment	Depreciation	Net Investment
1970–1974	27.1	13.2	13.8
1975–1979	32.0	15.9	16.1
1980–1984	30.8	19.0	11.9
1985	34.4	21.1	13.3
1986	34.6	21.9	12.6
1987	33.4	22.6	10.7
1988a	34.8	23.5	11.3
1989a	34.1	24.3	9.8

a = preliminary data
SOURCE: U.S. Office of Management and Budget, *Special Analyses: Budget of the United States Government, Fiscal Year 1989* (Washington, D.C.: Government Printing Office, 1988), table D-4. Data refer to fiscal years.

ately, it also credits the federal account for asset sales. Such sales are included as a revenue item, so they reduce the deficit just as tax receipts do. The transactions are fundamentally different, however: with asset sales, the government is trading one asset for another, with no effect on its net worth. While these sales are not large enough to reverse basic inferences about the nature of the deficit, they yield a somewhat optimistic account of recent federal fiscal actions. (See also note to table 1–4.)

Other intergenerational transfers. Intergenerational transfers are a central issue of deficit policy. None of the deficit measures presented above, however, provides a complete summary of the effects of fiscal policy on different generations. A deficit-financed increase in non-durable government outlays benefits all generations alive at the time of the expenditure, but the associated taxes are levied on those who are alive in future periods. The federal government may also transfer resources across generations without any changes in measured deficits.[5]

The 1983 social security reforms provide a clear example of intergenerational transfers that are not reflected in the deficit. If these reforms are phased in as scheduled between now and 1997, they will raise the retirement age and increase the payroll tax for current workers. These reforms induce substantial transfers from workers in the baby boom generation to subsequent generations, who would otherwise have had to provide for the baby boomers' generous retirement benefits.

Another example of intergenerational transfers other than the budget is the institution of tax policies that affect the value of existing assets (hence changing the price at which the current young generations can purchase them for the currently old). The Tax Reform Act of 1986, for example, reduced tax burdens on existing corporate assets by lowering the corporate tax rate, while it eliminated many investment incentives and therefore lowered the steady-state capital stock. This policy provided a windfall to the current asset holders, financed in part with an implicit tax on future generations in the form of lower capital accumulation.

Although expenditure and tax programs have important effects on the government's total intergenerational wealth transfers, they do not make deficits a useless measure of fiscal policy. In periods without many other reforms in fiscal stance, the measured deficit provides a reasonable guide to intergenerational fiscal policy.

State and local surpluses. Table 1–6 summarizes the history of federal, state–local, and total government deficits during the past three decades. The data show that the pattern of the early 1980s,

TABLE 1–6
STATE, LOCAL, AND FEDERAL DEFICITS AS A PERCENTAGE
OF GNP, 1950–1988

	Federal Deficit-Surplus	State-Local Deficit-Surplus	Total Government Deficit-Surplus
1950s	0.1	−0.2	−0.1
1960s	−0.3	0.0	−0.3
1970s	−1.7	0.8	−1.0
1980–1988	−3.9	1.3	−2.6
1980	−2.2	1.0	−1.3
1981	−2.1	1.1	−1.0
1982	−4.6	1.1	−3.5
1983	−5.2	1.4	−3.8
1984	−4.5	1.7	−2.8
1985	−4.9	1.6	−3.3
1986	−4.9	1.5	−3.4
1987	−3.6	1.1	−2.4
1988	−3.0	1.0	−2.0

SOURCE: National Income and Product Accounts, tables 3.2 and 3.3, and authors' calculations.

when total government deficits were smaller than the federal deficit, was reversed in the late 1980s. State and local surpluses as a share of GNP began to decline in 1984, and by 1988 these surpluses were less than 1 percent of GNP above their average level in the 1970s. The state–local fiscal position therefore does not reverse the broad pattern of increased deficits during the 1980s observed in the earlier tables.

Measurement issues aside, there are two important reasons for focusing on federal, rather than total, government deficits. First, much of the state–local surplus reflects contributions to state and local retirement funds. These accounts offset accruing liabilities of state and local governments to their employees.

Second, the economic mechanism by which state–local deficits affect the economy differs from that for federal deficits, because labor and capital are mobile across jurisdictions. Land prices in different communities can respond to differences in expected future tax burdens. Residents of a town that finances a new bridge with debt will discover that their house prices have fallen as new buyers discount the future tax liabilities. Residents may be indifferent between debt and tax finance as a result. The lower degree of factor mobility between nations reduces the scope for similar capitalization effects with regard to the federal debt.

Implicit federal liabilities. Yet another objection to the debt and deficit measures reported above is that they ignore changing implicit liabilities of the federal government. Standard calculations measure direct federal borrowing—the real value of publicly held federal debt—but they omit both government loan guarantees and borrowing by government-sponsored enterprises; both types of borrowing are increasingly important.

Examples of government loan guarantees include federally guaranteed mortgages through the Federal Housing Administration and the Veterans Administration, guaranteed student loans, and subsidies for export sales through the Commodity Credit Corporation. In fiscal 1988, the net change in outstanding guaranteed loans was $20.8 billion. The stock of outstanding federally guaranteed debt at the end of fiscal 1988 was $527.8 billion, or 26 percent of federal debt held by the public.

Federal credit guarantees impose a liability on the government, but they are less burdensome than ordinary borrowing since in most cases the homeowner, farmer, or other borrower will actually repay the loan without any need for federal intervention. The default rate for student loans, for example, is currently 9 percent. The cost of these programs should be measured in the way an actuary measures the liabilities of an insurance company, by projecting the govern-

14

ment's expected liability for the guaranteed loans. Current budgetary practice ignores these liabilities, however, until losses actually occur. Since these loans are concentrated in sectors such as agriculture and housing, a large federal outflow through these programs is a nontrivial risk in some future year. Current accrual accounting procedures ignore this possibility.[6]

Government-sponsored enterprises (GSEs) are the second category of federal credit activity excluded from traditional debt measures. These include the Federal National Mortgage Corporation, the Federal Home Loan Mortgage Corporation, the Federal Agricultural Mortgage Corporation, and a variety of other institutions designed to channel credit to particular sectors of the economy. GSE loans outstanding at the end of fiscal 1988 totaled $673.4 billion, or 33 percent of the publicly held federal debt.[7] While these loans are not explicitly backed by the federal government, default by major GSEs would have extremely disruptive effects on the credit markets and on important sectors of the U.S. economy.

The precise status of these loans is uncertain, and in the event of default the federal government would have no statutory liability to back the debt. The economic dislocation associated with widespread defaults on the loans in these pools would, however, lead to calls for federal intervention and support. These implicit liabilities are therefore even more difficult to value than those associated with explicitly guaranteed loans. Since the current tight-budget atmosphere in Washington is certain to lead to further use of these off-budget agencies to finance new government initiatives, they should be recognized as a partial component of federal borrowing.

Asset revaluations and federal net worth. Since the federal government owns vast land areas, for example, and holds development rights for oil and other minerals, year-to-year changes in commodity prices can often swamp the more gradual changes in tax or expenditure policy.

While recognizing that the real value of federal assets is important for logical consistency with our measurement of the real federal debt, it is not clear how such price changes should be treated in measuring the deficit. The oil price example is helpful in this context. When oil prices rise, assets held by the federal government increase in value. At the same time, the cost of future government services increases because the government is a substantial purchaser of gasoline for military and other purposes. The correct accounting for such a price change would therefore recognize both the current asset effect as well as the future price effect, which is difficult to calculate.

15

Whether including only the current asset effect makes adjusted deficit measures more or less reliable as a guide to fiscal policy is unclear.

Short-Run Deficit Outlook. During the past decade, the federal deficit, measured by the Congressional Budget Office as a share of GNP, peaked at 6.3 percent in 1983. By 1988 it was three percentage points lower, and current forecasts call for continued gradual reduction. The most widely cited forecasts are provided by the Congressional Budget Office. Its expenditure forecasts assume that no new spending programs will be enacted between now and 1994. Discussions of a renewed U.S. interplanetary space program, calls for new initiatives to improve public infrastructure, and the prospect of other new outlays make these forecasts regarding nondefense outlays conservative.

International Comparisons

The U.S. deficit experience of the past decade is not unique. The 1980s witnessed the growth of public debt ratios worldwide. In the 1970s, debt ratios in most countries moved relatively little. Large deficits and debt creation were matched by inflationary growth of nominal incomes. In the 1980s, by contrast, large deficits and sharply higher real interest rates reversed debt dynamics to produce an explosion of debt ratios. This chapter contrasts recent U.S. fiscal experience with that of other large industrial nations. The analysis shows that the American experience during the early 1980s was similar to that of other countries, but that the United States has reduced the noninterest federal deficit less rapidly than other nations during more recent years.

In table 1–7 we show the debt and deficit data for a number of individual European countries, the United States, and Japan. Table 1–7 highlights three important facts:

• There was an unambiguous pattern of increased debt ratios in the 1980s with only two exceptions, Luxembourg and the United Kingdom.

• There was a shift during the past decade to *large* noninterest budget *surplus*. In fact, Italy is the only country in the group that did not run a primary or noninterest surplus by 1989.

• Although most countries experienced noninterest surpluses by 1989, the overall budget remained in deficit with four exceptions, Denmark, Japan, Luxembourg, and the United Kingdom.

The shift has been toward more conservative public finance in industrialized countries. The 1960s legitimized deficit finance, and

TABLE 1–7

GROSS PUBLIC DEBT AND DEFICITS IN EUROPE, THE UNITED STATES,
AND JAPAN AS A PERCENTAGE OF GDP, 1981 AND 1988

	1981			1988		
	Debt	Total deficit	Primary deficit	Debt	Total deficit	Primary deficit
Europe	40.6	3.8	1.4	58.7	2.9	−1.8
Belgium	75.7	12.6	4.8	126.5	5.9	−4.5
Denmark	39.3	6.9	1.6	62.5	−1.0	−8.5
France	24.6	1.9	−0.1	36.5	1.7	−1.1
Germany	32.7	3.7	1.4	44.7	0.8	−2.0
Greece	28.8	11.0	7.9	73.6	12.8	3.2
Ireland	76.8	13.4	6.8	118.6	5.1	−4.3
Italy	58.5	11.3	5.2	94.1	9.9	1.0
Luxembourg	13.6	3.6	2.7	10.0	−5.6	−6.7
Netherlands	45.9	5.5	1.0	78.5	4.5	−1.5
Portugal	37.1	9.2	4.1	72.2	6.1	−2.4
Spain	18.2	3.9	3.1	47.7	3.2	−0.3
United Kingdom	52.3	2.6	2.4	48.6	−1.2	−4.7
United States	37.1	1.0	0.7	51.5	1.7	0.3
Japan	57.1	3.9	2.5	68.3	−0.2	−2.8

NOTE: The primary budget deficit excludes interest payments. A minus (−)
sign denotes a surplus.
SOURCES: European Community, *European Economy* (Brussels), various issues.

the 1970s allowed it to go haywire; in the 1980s fiscal restraint has
been the rule in Europe. Countries where debt ratios are extreme,
like Italy, Ireland, and Belgium, are under considerable pressure to
bring deficits under control to avoid becoming a source of financial
instability. The reduction in the primary budget deficit goes in that
direction but certainly not far enough in Italy to make up for substantial debt service.

The debt ratios of the United States, Europe, and Japan do not
differ significantly. In fact, the U.S. debt ratio is lower than the
European average or that of Japan. In most industrialized countries
the debt ratio has stabilized. After rising during the first part of the
1980s, the debt-to-GNP ratio is now basically constant at a higher
level.

The international evidence draws attention to important measurement issues raised in chapter 2. Different organizations report
quite different debt ratios, and a central issue in international com-

parisons is whether to look at gross or net debt, that is, whether to make an offset against debt for government assets. Such a distinction is particularly important if the debt has a substantial counterpart in public sector real assets, including assets that yield cash revenues. Table 1–8 shows Organization for Economic Cooperation and Development (OECD) data for gross and net debt of the general government for four countries. The two debt measures show the same trends, but their levels differ significantly, especially in the case of Japan. On the whole, though, neither gross nor net debt ratios show the United States as a special case.

Deficit Experience. Although the debt ratios across nations move together, the deficit experience across countries differs. Europe and Japan have substantial primary or noninterest surpluses, whereas the United States has a modest noninterest deficit. This is evident from the 1988 data presented in table 1–7. The United States is not an outlier, however. The extremes are between the United Kingdom, which is retiring debt, and Italy, where the debt ratio is rising rapidly.

Net real interest payments for different nations also suggest that the United States is not atypical. In the budgets of Europe, Japan, and the United States alike, the accumulation of debts has increased the share of interest payments in government outlays. Since inflation rates differ, an adjustment for the inflation component of nominal interest rates has to be made. Table 1–9 shows that for all countries except Japan real interest payments have become a more positive factor in the budget. In the United States, for example, the shift amounts to more than 2 percent of GDP. This shift reflects the combination of rising real interest rates and an increase in the debt ratio since 1980.

The U.S. experience differs from that of other countries in two

TABLE 1–8
GROSS AND NET GENERAL GOVERNMENT DEBT AS A PERCENTAGE OF
GNP, FOUR COUNTRIES, 1988

	Gross	Net
United States	51.5	30.6
Japan	68.3	22.6
Germany	44.6	23.5
United Kingdom	45.3	38.5

NOTE: "General government" refers to federal, state, and local government.
SOURCE: OECD, *Economic Outlook*, various issues.

TABLE 1–9

REAL GOVERNMENT INTEREST PAYMENTS AS A PERCENTAGE OF GDP,
1975–1980 AND 1988

	1975–1980	1988
United States	−1.1	1.0
Japan	2.1	1.0
Europe	−2.4	2.4
Germany	0.4	1.7
United Kingdom	−4.6	1.0

NOTE: A minus (−) sign denotes a surplus.
SOURCE: European Community, *European Economy* (Brussels), various issues.

ways. First, the absolute size of U.S. debts and deficits is huge, reflecting the relative size of the United States and individual other countries. Second, in the United States the dissaving of the public sector does not have a counterpart in a very high private saving rate. As a result there is national dissaving on a substantial scale. The United States is borrowing in world capital markets and net foreign assets have turned negative.

Deficits, Investment, and the Current Account

Deficits are charged with causing inflation, trade deficits, undersaving, and the productivity slowdown, and with raising the risk of various economic crises. Many of these charges are overblown. Deficits like those the United States has experienced in the past decade do not have dramatic effects on most aspects of the national economy. Doomsayers who point to certain economic calamity if the deficit is not corrected immediately are simply alarmists. Nevertheless, deficits do affect economic performance. There are important links between deficits, national saving, and our trade balance. Moreover, the effects of the higher level of national debt that deficits leave behind persist for many years. Deciding whether deficits constitute appropriate fiscal policy thus depends not only on their short-run effects, but also on their longer-term economic consequences.

The textbook "neoclassical" analysis of government deficits assumes that the economy is fully employed, so a deficit increase due to either higher government spending or reduced taxes cannot affect gross national product. We illustrate this analysis by considering a deficit that results from a tax cut: government outlays are held constant. The reduction in tax burdens provides additional disposable income to households, who will try to increase their consumption. Firms may also attempt to undertake additional investment if corporate taxes are lowered and some firms face cash-flow constraints, or if the tax reduction includes expanded investment incentives.

The fundamental national income identity divides the economy's output into four categories: consumption, investment, net exports, and government purchases. Since output and government purchases are fixed, the tax cut cannot change the sum of consumption, investment, and net exports. Economic conditions respond to the deficit so that there are offsetting negative effects on consumption, investment, and the trade balance.

The offset to increased consumption and investment demand occurs in two ways. First, interest rates rise. This lowers investment demand by firms, which face higher capital costs, and reduces consumption demand by households, which face more attractive saving opportunities. Whether the economy's total investment or total consumption declines may depend on the nature of the tax reduction. Second, to reduce net exports, the exchange rate appreciates. This makes foreign goods less expensive and encourages imports, while also reducing the competitiveness of domestic goods in foreign markets and thereby lowering exports.

In this standard view, a reduction in individual taxes without an offsetting change in government outlays would therefore reduce investment and lead to a current account deficit. A corporate tax reduction might raise investment, but it would lower consumption and also raise net imports.

There are two rejoinders to this standard analysis. The first, a traditional Keynesian argument,[8] takes issue with the assumption that the economy is operating at full employment. When a substantial share of the economy's labor or capital resources is underutilized, higher deficits may have expansionary effects. In this case, the sum of consumption, investment, and net exports need not be constant: it may actually increase as national output rises. Deficits may raise consumption and investment, although they are still likely to worsen the current account as higher domestic income encourages imports.

Whether the Keynesian analysis applies to a given deficit episode depends on the macroeconomic circumstances. For the 1930s and even the early 1980s, this is quite likely to be the relevant model for analyzing deficits. The case for applying the Keynesian view to the deficits of the late 1980s, however, when the economy had been operating at or near full employment for several years, was quite weak.

Ricardian Equivalence—The Rejoinder That Will Not Die

A second rejoinder to the standard analysis, and one that has attracted substantial academic research during the past decade, disputes the central claim that a tax reduction that widens the deficit will raise household consumption. According to this "Ricardian equivalence" view,[9] households recognize that when taxes are reduced but the government maintains its expenditure level, higher future taxes will be associated with the borrowing that finances current outlays. Government debt therefore does not contribute to the household sector's net worth and does not affect consumption.

Government bonds are an asset to their holders, but they are simultaneously a liability to the taxpayers who must ultimately redeem them. The Ricardian view holds that these assets and liabilities cancel each other, so in the absence of distributional effects, changes in the level of government debt should not affect total spending.

The principal counterargument to the Ricardian view, which suggests that debt does represent net wealth, holds that debt is an asset of current generations while the tax burdens that will repay this debt are a liability of future generations.[10] To the extent that budget deficits, which lead to debt accumulation by the current generation, make current consumers feel better off, their effects on total spending may be positive.

The proposition that deficits transfer tax burdens to future taxpayers is uncontroversial. Whether these transfers raise expenditures by current taxpayers is less clear, however. Two arguments can be advanced in this vein. First, most government debt is repaid relatively quickly. Much of the burden of repaying the debt incurred in typical deficit episodes therefore falls on those who are alive during the deficit period, so the view that deficits transfer taxes to "future generations" is an exaggeration.[11] Deficits largely alter the timing of taxes during the lifetime of those alive during the tax cut. As we illustrated in table 1–1, the debt-to-GNP ratio declined by more than 50 percent in the decade after World War II. Nearly half of the government debt incurred during the war was effectively repaid within this period.

A second argument against the view that transferring tax liabilities to future generations raises current spending is that such fiscal transfers may be offset by private intergenerational transfers, as parents leave larger bequests to enable their children to pay higher taxes.[12] A substantial part of the recent academic debate on the burden of the debt has focused on the importance of intergenerational transfers, particularly on whether bequest motives give current households effectively infinite horizons with respect to tax burdens.

21

The relatively rapid repayment of most government debt makes such transfer motives a second-order issue for assessing the short-run effects of government deficits on national saving, although bequest issues are central to evaluating the long-run effects of deficits.

The debate on how deficits affect current consumption is not yet settled, but there are several reasons for suspecting that tax reductions are not fully offset by private saving and therefore do reduce national saving. First, liquidity constraints may link current income to consumption for some households. Government deficits, which in effect allow consumers to borrow by deferring taxes, therefore increase spending. Available empirical evidence suggests that a nontrivial fraction of households may face liquidity constraints. Micro-econometric studies of spending decisions suggest that households with low net worth exhibit greater sensitivity of consumption to income fluctuations than the life cycle–permanent income model would suggest. Other studies find that over the lifetime, consumption and income are highly correlated, suggesting that even expected income fluctuations may affect consumption.[13]

The presence of liquidity constraints does not necessarily imply that changes in fiscal policy will affect consumption, since a household's access to credit may be affected by the government's deficit policy. If liquidity constraints arise because of difficulties in enforcing some debt contracts (such as the inability to place liens on social security and some other transfer payments), then the presence of these constraints will link consumer spending to fiscal policy.[14]

A second reason for suspecting imperfect private offset to government deficits is consumer myopia. Households may fail to make rational forecasts of their future incomes, may not recognize future and sometimes implicit tax liabilities they will face, or may simply misestimate future needs in formulating their consumption plans. Many studies of household purchases of durable goods, for example, suggest implicit discount rates of 25–35 percent per year in household behavior.[15] Such discount rates would lead to substantial consumption changes when taxes are reduced, even if the tax cut were to be reversed several years later.

Third, households might believe that growth rates are high enough, and interest rates low enough, that the government will never need to raise future taxes to finance increased indebtedness. A steady-state growth rate above the real interest rate would be sufficient for this view. In this case, consumers may treat government debt as net wealth and therefore increase their consumption. Since the marginal propensity to consume from wealth is relatively low, however—perhaps three cents of additional spending for each one dollar increase in wealth—this effect is likely to be smaller than the consumption increase associated with either liquidity constraints or myopia.

Each of the three foregoing arguments undermines a premise of the Ricardian equivalence argument, thereby casting doubt on the conclusion. Another line of argument, however, uses the premises of the Ricardian argument to derive other implausible results, and therefore concludes that the premises must be violated in some dimension. The clearest example is the argument that the links between generations in the Ricardian model are so strong that they also imply that many transfers within generations—such as those associated with typical distortional taxes—have no effect because different individuals in the current generation are linked by the future marriages of their offspring.[16] Since there is ample evidence that transfers and other programs that redistribute resources within generations affect spending, the results, while still controversial, cast doubt on the strong Ricardian view.

Despite its influence on the path of academic research, the Ricardian view that deficits are of no consequence has not percolated into the political process.[17] Politicians behave as though taxing current generations is more costly than taxing future generations. This sentiment probably reflects the views of voters and therefore raises yet another objection to the irrelevance position.

Empirical Evidence

Despite numerous statistical studies using data for the United States and other countries, there is no consensus on how government deficits affect national saving, interest rates, or the current account.

Valid econometric experiments for analyzing how deficits affect real activity are difficult to find. Much of the variation in government deficits, both through time in a given country and across nations, is due to the variation in cyclical conditions or to other special events such as the outbreak of wars. Neither provides a valid experiment for studying how deficits affect real activity. Cyclical variation proves difficult because many aspects of economic activity change over the business cycle, and there is a danger of incorrectly associating these changes with the deficit. Similarly, military conflicts distort the economy, reducing consumption and thereby biasing the results toward finding higher personal saving when deficits expand.

The 1980s provide one of the best historical experiments for analyzing how deficits affect economic activity, because the recent deficits are not associated with military activity and span a number of years with different macroeconomic conditions. This experience suggests that deficits raise real interest rates, lower national saving, and induce a current account imbalance.

The Congressional Budget Office has recently surveyed the evidence and concludes as follows:

> Most of the single-equation studies that test for statistical relations found a positive, if small, relationship between deficits or debt and interest rates. On average the 25 studies analyzed by the Congressional Budget Office suggest that, other things remaining equal, a $50 billion deficit reduction would lead to a fall in the short-term interest rate of 0.1 percentage point after one year.[18]

International Aspects of Recent U.S. Fiscal Policy

The international perspective on recent fiscal policy raises two questions:

- What are the reasons for the trade deficit? Is it mostly a reflection of the overvalued dollar in the 1980–1985 period, and is its persistence a reflection of very slow adjustment to the gain in competitiveness? Or are there important structural reasons for the trade deficit? These might be found in either the domestic macroeconomy or changing trends in world trade.
- If budget adjustment does take place, will it be primarily reflected in higher investment or in a reduced external balance? In a closed economy investment would be crowded in by budget cuts, but that need not be the case in an open economy.

Twin Deficits of the 1980s. It is useful to begin with a classification of sources of external imbalance. A point of departure in classifying deficits is the national income accounts identity:

$$\text{Current Account} = \text{National Saving} - \text{Investment}$$

Because this is an identity, an external deficit reflects an excess of spending over income or of investment over saving. Changes in the budget are among the possible disturbances.

In early 1989 the U.S. merchandise trade deficit at an annual rate amounted to $107 billion, down from the more than $150 billion in 1986. The broader measure of the current account, including not only merchandise trade but also services and investment income, showed a deficit of $124 billion. While this deficit, too, had declined over the past year from a peak of $160 billion, it was actually back on the rise. In figure 1–3 the current account data are shown as a fraction of GNP. Forecasts for the U.S. economic balance do not show significant improvement in the next three years. For example, DRI/McGraw Hill

24

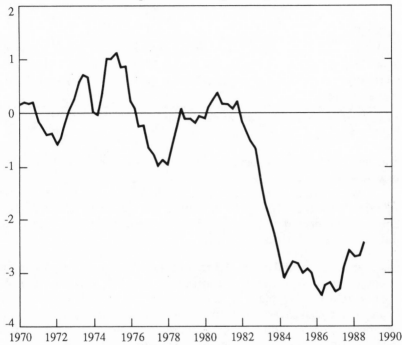

FIGURE 1–3
U.S. CURRENT ACCOUNT–GNP, 1970–1988
(third quarter moving average)

SOURCE: Author.

predicts that by 1992 both the current account and the trade deficit
will still exceed $100 billion.

There is no presumption that current accounts should be balanced in the short run or even over extended periods of time, and in
fact they have not been, as table 1–10 shows. But it is essential to
know whether these deficits are "productive" or whether they mostly
reflect postponement of necessary adjustment.

There are many explanations for external imbalances. They include improved investment opportunities, demographic influences
on saving or investment, and adjustment to increased financial inter-
mediation which eases borrowing constraints, transitory effects of
terms of trade shocks or structural adjustment to changing trends in
world markets, and changes in public finance (in the absence of
Ricardian equivalence). In the United States, public finance is clearly
not the only reason for the current account deficit: the national saving

25

TABLE 1–10
External Imbalances

	1960–1979	1980–1987
Australia	−1.7	−4.5
Canada	0.4	−0.3
Japan	0.5	2.1
Germany	0.8	1.3
United States	0.6	−1.8

NOTE: Data are current account as percentage of GDP.
SOURCE: OECD.

rate has declined as a result of both the deficit and the fall in the private saving rate.

It is equally true, however, that public sector dissaving is at least in part a reason for the external deficit. The extent to which budget deficits are reflected in external deficits depends on the integration of the world capital market.

International Capital Market Integration. The United States is an open economy. It is therefore appropriate to ask in what way crowding out, if any, takes place in an open economy. In a closed economy a fall in saving will be reflected in a decline in investment. An open economy offers an additional possibility, namely, a deterioration in the current account or financing of investment by foreign saving. Which of the two channels predominates? The question is of interest not only in interpreting the experience of the 1980s but also, looking ahead, in knowing whether budget cuts translate into trade improvement or into increased *domestic* investment.

The standard answer is that world capital markets are integrated and that real interest rates cannot move far apart internationally over any significant period of time. This leads to the conclusion that real exchange rate changes would have to do at least part and perhaps most of the crowding in of demand. An entirely different view on this subject has been developed by Feldstein[19] and the implications of his research are altogether striking.

Feldstein discovered a tight link between national saving and investment rates. On latest estimates three-quarters of the increase in saving would be retained in higher investment and only one-quarter would flow out. That implies that U.S. budget cutting has only minor current account effects and primarily raises investment.

The finding continues to be debated, but the striking saving-investment correlation is no longer in question. What is in question is the interpretation. The most plausible story is that capital markets work on two levels: there is a wholesale market which is intensely integrated at the international level, and a retail market which has few if any linkages. A good example might be the U.S. housing market. In the 1960s U.S. housing was dominantly intermediated by *local* savings and loan institutions, which attracted *local* deposits and made *local* housing loans. This housing finance was virtually non-traded. Today housing loans are administered by local financial institutions, but the homogeneous claims are traded nationally, packaged for the wholesale market. As a result of deregulation, saving from anywhere can go to housing investment anywhere.

The high correlation of saving and investment within countries suggests that the world capital market is *extremely* segmented. This is, of course, a very striking suggestion, since all casual evidence points in exactly the other direction: intense speculation across borders at the slightest sign of capital gains. But the housing example is useful because in the U.S. capital market of the 1970s nontraded mortgages clearly coexisted with a highly efficient wholesale market.

If the high correlation reflects primarily nontraded credit, there is another striking implication: financial deregulation and competition will give low-saving countries access to the saving pool of high-saving regions. As a result the world economy will operate more in allocating credit by interest rates and world credit rating and less by local availability.

In conclusion, there is ambiguity about the effects of budget cutting on the external balance and on investment. The exact distribution between the two adjustments is not known and the channels and mechanisms may be in the midst of profound transformation. Budget cutting will probably result in some combination of lower external deficits and higher investment, both of which are desirable. The exact division not only depends on capital mobility or capital market integration, but also is affected significantly by the fiscal and monetary policies adopted abroad.

Deficits and Social Security

Deficits and social security policy are the federal government's two most powerful instruments for redistributing resources across generations, and they should be evaluated with reference to each other. The budget deficits of the past decade place additional tax burdens on the taxpayers of the next century, the same taxpayers who will be responsible for financing the retirement pensions of the baby boom generation. These burdens are compounded because the social secur-

27

ity and Medicare systems are projected to experience large deficits when the baby boomers reach retirement age.

Deficit Accounting and Social Security. The 1983 social security reforms raised payroll taxes by enough to generate a surplus in the social security trust fund beginning in 1985. Federal accounting conventions combine the surplus or deficit from this trust fund, known as an "off budget" surplus, with the "on budget" surplus or deficit from other federal operations, in calculating the total budget deficit. Trust fund surpluses therefore reduce the measured federal deficit.

The importance of these trust funds is shown in table 1–11.

The accounting procedure for calculating the off-budget social security surplus overstates the excess of taxes over benefits for the trust fund. In 1989, for example, the trust fund tax receipts were $267 billion, while benefit payments were $227 billion. The trust fund also

TABLE 1–11

SOCIAL SECURITY SURPLUSES AND THE BUDGET DEFICIT,
FISCAL YEARS 1980–1994

	Deficit Excluding Social Security	Social Security Surplus	Combined Deficit
1980	73	(1)	74
1981	74	(5)	79
1982	120	(8)	128
1983	108	0	208
1984	186	0	185
1985	222	10	212
1986	238	17	221
1987	169	19	150
1988	194	39	155
Forecasts			
1989	211	56	155 (136)
1990	209	68	141 (100)
1991	219	79	140 (64)
1992	225	90	135 (28)
1993	233	103	129 (0)
1994	239	117	122 (?)

SOURCE: Congressional Budget Office, *The Economic and Budget Outlook,* January 1989. Gramm-Rudman deficit targets are shown in parentheses.

spent $5 billion on administration, so the net surplus measured as taxes less outlays was $35 billion. Yet the reported off-budget surplus was $56 billion. The reconciliation between these values involves several intergovernmental transfers. Since trust fund revenues have exceeded outflows since 1985, the trust fund has accumulated interest bearing Treasury securities. In 1989, the trust fund received $10 billion in net interest payments from the Treasury. Social security also collected $12 billion in transfers from other federal agencies, such as contributions on behalf of their employees. Receipts from other parts of the federal government are treated as "negative outlays," so the reported off-budget surplus is $56 ($35 + $10 + $12) billion.[20] Even focusing only on the smaller direct surplus, the $35 billion of tax receipts above outlays and expenses, the social security trust funds are a key component of the narrowing deficit.

The social security surpluses raise a deeper question, however: should contributions and withdrawals from trust funds be treated differently from other federal revenues and outlays in computing the deficit? The economic case for distinguishing the different components of the budget is weak. If the deficit is designed to measure the federal government's net contribution to economic stimulus in a given period, for example, then the level of tax collections is more important than their composition in determining fiscal stimulus. Whether the government collects more revenue because of higher payroll (social security) tax or higher income taxes, a tax increase will have a contractionary effect.

Some view social security as different from other federal programs because it is simply a system of savings accounts for its participants. This view neglects the actual experience of the social security system. The generous benefit increases of the 1970s, which raised the payouts to those who retired during the 1970s and 1980s well above the present value of their contributions, and the prospective benefit reductions and higher taxes on baby boomers in the 1983 reforms amply demonstrate that the social security system can deviate significantly from an actuarially fair saving and insurance scheme. When the system is viewed as a tax-and-transfer program for intergenerational redistribution, there is hardly an a priori case for special budgetary treatment.

Merely replacing the total deficit targets in the current legislation with the on-budget deficit has substantial appeal for the middle and late 1990s. Although forcing Congress to raise an additional $50 billion in revenue in each of the next few years, or find equally large spending cuts, would lead to substantial budgetary disruption, the longer-term goal of balancing on-budget outlays and revenues would

29

make the federal government a net saver. Because congressional budgeting decisions are clearly affected by the budget targets, this relabeling of the targets would have real effects on spending and revenue decisions.

Deficits, Social Security, and the Aging Population. The population cohort born between 1945 and 1964—the baby boom—is substantially larger than the cohort that follows it. Table 1–12 illustrates the importance of this demographic pattern for transfer programs that target the elderly population.

Until the past decade, the social security system operated on a pay-as-you-go (PAYG) basis. Payroll taxes, which are the system's only revenue source, were set roughly to equate tax receipts and benefit outflows. It became clear both that prevailing payroll tax rates would render the system bankrupt in the near future and that a solvent PAYG system would place high tax burdens on working households in the next century to finance transfers to the retired baby boomers. These required PAYG tax rates are shown in the third column of table 1–12.

TABLE 1–12
DEMOGRAPHIC CHANGE AND DEPENDENCY RATIOS, 1960–2050

	Population 65 +/ Population 20–64	OASDI Recipients/ Covered Worker	PAYG Payroll Tax Rate
1960	17.3	20	—
1970	18.5	27	—
1980	19.5	31	—
1990	21.0	30	12.1
2000	21.5	31	11.9
2010	22.3	34	12.0
2020	29.2	42	12.2
2030	37.8	50	12.3
2040	39.1	52	16.8
2050	39.7	53	16.4

NOTE: OASDI = old-age, survivors, and disability insurance; PAYG = pay-as-you-go.
SOURCE: *1988 Annual Report of the Board of Trustees of the Federal Old-Age and Survivors Insurance and Disability Insurance Trust Funds* (Baltimore: Social Security Administration, 1988). Column 1 is from p. 93, column 2 from p. 80. Column 3 is drawn from Robert P. Hagemann and Giuseppe Nicoletti, "Population Aging: Economic Effects and Some Policy Implications for Financing Public Pensions," *OECD Economic Studies*, no. 12 (Spring 1989), p. 70.

The reforms raised payroll tax rates, which currently stand at 15.3 percent, and prospectively increased the social security retirement age from 65 to 67. The net effect of these changes is that for the next twenty-five years, social security taxes are projected to exceed benefit outflows and to result in accumulation of a substantial social security trust fund, which can subsequently be used for benefit payments to baby boomers.

The upper half of table 1–13 shows the time profile of taxes and benefit payouts for social security. The projected time profile of taxes and benefits leads to accumulation of substantial reserves in the social security trust fund. Table 1–14 shows that by the year 2020, the projections call for assets of $9.4 trillion, or nearly 30 percent of GNP.

TABLE 1–13

FINANCES OF SOCIAL SECURITY AND MEDICARE SYSTEMS AS
PERCENTAGE OF GNP, 1988–2050

	Expenses	Taxes	Surplus/Deficit
Social Security			
1988	4.7	5.4	0.7
1990	4.7	5.4	0.7
1995	4.6	5.4	0.8
2000	4.5	5.5	1.0
2010	4.6	5.4	0.8
2020	5.6	5.4	−0.2
2030	6.5	5.4	−1.1
2040	6.5	5.4	−1.1
Social Security and Hospital Insurance			
1988	5.8	6.7	0.9
1990	5.9	6.8	0.9
1995	6.0	6.8	0.8
2000	6.0	6.5	0.5
2010	6.3	6.7	0.4
2020	7.8	6.7	−1.1
2030	9.2	6.6	−2.6
2040	9.3	6.5	−2.8
2050	9.3	6.4	−2.9

SOURCE: *1988 Annual Report of the Board of Trustees of the Federal Old-Age and Survivors Insurance and Federal Disability Insurance Trust Funds* (Baltimore: Social Security Administration, 1988), Table F1. Projections are based on the demographic and economic assumptions in "Scenario II-B."

TABLE 1–14
Social Security Trust Fund Accumulation, 1990–2050

	Trust Fund Assets (Current Dollars, Billions)	As Percentage of GNP
1990	200	3.7
2000	1,290	12.7
2010	4,490	24.5
2020	9,390	29.7
2030	12,410	22.8
2040	10,680	11.2
2050	780	0.5

Source: John C. Hambor, "Economic Policy, Intergenerational Equity, and the Social Security Trust Fund Buildup," Social Security Bulletin no. 50, October 1987, p. 14.

Accumulating trust fund surpluses for both social security and hospital insurance affects intergenerational redistribution in two ways. First, assets in the trust fund reduce the payroll tax rate needed to finance projected outlays. Second, government saving while the baby boomers are working increases the capital stock available to their children, thereby raising national income when the boomers reach retirement.

The future of the social security trust fund and its net effect on national saving depends critically on future policy actions. If the reserves are allowed to accumulate undisturbed and their presence does not discourage deficit reduction on other accounts, the trust fund would acquire virtually all of the outstanding federal debt by 2020.

The frequent claim that the United States needs to save more on account of recent and prospective demographic changes is at least overstated, and is probably incorrect. *Ceteris paribus*, an economy that saves optimally and responds optimally to a demographic shift like that experienced in the United States during the last quarter century, would *lower*, not raise, its national saving rate. This is because lower fertility, which eventually leads to higher dependency burdens, generates slower labor force growth rates *before* the increased dependence. This reduces the share of national income that must be invested to maintain any given level of capital intensity, freeing resources for consumption. It also leads to fewer dependent children as a share of the population; this short-run reduction in consumption-needs partly offsets the long-run trend toward more dependent elderly.

Slower labor force growth and declining numbers of youthful dependents raise consumption opportunities for the next few decades.[21] While other factors may justify raising the national saving rate above recent U.S. experience, the anticipated demographic shift does not provide strong support for this position. If national saving is too low, however, accumulation of a social security trust fund may nevertheless be a politically expedient way of raising the national saving rate. In a second scenario, the continuing combination of the surplus from social security with the on-budget deficit for accounting purposes leads to ongoing federal deficits. The accumulation of trust fund reserves is therefore partly matched by growing federal debt and potential social security benefit increases during the next two decades. The result is a smaller trust fund when the baby boomers reach retirement. The result in this scenario is likely to be a scaling back of social security benefits, in conjunction with a higher tax rate on employed households. This scenario would involve transfers to those who retire in the early twenty-first century and away from both the baby boomers, whose higher payroll taxes finance both greater social security benefits and greater government outlays for this group, and the children of the baby boomers, who must then finance their parents' retirement.

While the frequent claim that demographic factors require the accumulation of a large social security trust fund is overstated, social security policy is a central determinant of federal fiscal stance. Payroll tax increases during the mid-1980s helped slow the growth of total federal deficits, but as the political debate surrounding Senator Moynihan's 1990 payroll tax cut suggests, this component of fiscal restraint may be transient.

What Is to Be Done?

Government deficits are not necessarily bad. In some circumstances a government would be irresponsible not to spend more than it receives.

The National Saving Problem. Budget deficits affect economic activity by reducing national saving. In the long run, a nation's saving rate determines the level of investment it can undertake, so low saving translates into a smaller capital stock and slower growth in living standards. While the Ricardian view of deficits predicts that private saving should increase when the government dissaves, it is not supported by the history of the past decade. Instead, high deficits coincided with depressed private saving. Rather than offsetting the economic effects of the deficit, lower private saving amplifies these effects.

33

Table 1–15 reports the U.S. national saving rate, as well as its public and private saving components, for 1950 through 1988. From 8.6 percent of NNP in the 1960s, the saving rate fell to 7.8 percent during the 1970s and only 2.3 percent during the second half of the 1980s. Table 1–15 shows that the national saving decline during the past decade is not solely the result of government dissaving: private saving also declined during this period.

Persistently low national saving translates into reduced investment. The link between reduced saving and reduced investment can be broken in the short run, however, by international capital flows. A nation's current account deficit equals the difference between its saving and investment rates. Countries investing more than they are saving therefore must borrow funds from abroad. To obtain these foreign funds, such low-saving nations must import more goods than they export. The decline in the U.S. national saving rate during the 1980s is thus the proximate cause of the deterioration in the U.S. trade balance.

Net investment in the United States has not declined by as much as the saving rate. When saving is scarce, interest rates and required equity returns must increase to ration the supply of capital. Lower national saving in the United States than in its competitors raises the cost of capital to U.S. firms. For example, a number of recent studies comparing the costs of capital facing U.S. and Japanese firms suggest that Japan's cost of capital is lower than that of the United States; in the early 1980s this was the result of the apparently lower cost of debt finance, but recently the cost of equity appears to be an important driving force.[22]

Continuation of the current depressed rate of national saving will eventually slow the growth of living standards in the United

TABLE 1–15

COMPONENTS OF NATIONAL SAVING AS PERCENTAGE OF NNP, 1950–1988

	Private Saving	Government Saving	National Saving
1950s	8.3	−0.2	8.1
1960s	8.9	−0.3	8.6
1970s	8.9	−1.1	7.8
1980–1988	6.3	−2.9	3.4
1985–1988	5.4	−3.1	2.3

SOURCE: National Income and Product Accounts.

States relative to those abroad. If foreigners eventually choose to supply less capital to the American economy, for risk or other reasons, real wages will decline as the capital-labor ratio falls. Even if the needed capital is provided by overseas investors, the returns to such capital investments will no longer be part of domestic income. Rather, they will accrue to the foreign investors and therefore will not contribute to boosting national income in the same way that domestically owned capital would.

There are two reasons not to postpone actions to raise national saving:

First, borrowing today accumulates debts. The interest on these debts—whether incurred by the government or by private firms—will ultimately have to be paid by a reduction in the standard of living. Since there is no reason to expect that the debts will simply vanish, by inflation or otherwise, it is appropriate to start adjustment as early as possible. This argument is reinforced by the fact that the high value of the dollar associated with our current monetary-fiscal mix promotes deindustrialization. When adjustment comes, the decline in the standard of living will be larger because we will not have invested in those activities that earn foreign exchange.

The second argument for early adjustment draws attention to the risk of a funding crisis. For the time being there is no sign of any reluctance of the rest of the world to continue financing our trade imbalances, but that situation can change from one day to the next, as indeed happened in the Carter administration. A rapid change in foreign confidence, or merely a foreign belief that we might not keep interest rates high enough to reward the risks of holding an overvalued asset, can turn asset markets in no time. Unlimited dollar selling could then easily translate into a major dollar fall, with potential repercussions throughout the world financial system. The longer the United States continues as a low-saving nation, the greater the risk of such an outcome.

Raising National Saving: Private Saving Options. The national saving rate can be increased either by raising private saving or by reducing government dissaving by federal deficit reduction. The latter is the more potent and reliable instrument; but given the political difficulties of raising taxes or reducing spending, we begin by discussing options to raise private saving.

Private saving can be raised either by encouraging individuals to consume less and save more, or by providing incentives for firms to retain a higher fraction of their after-tax profits. The most direct method of encouraging individual saving is to reduce the tax burden on investment income, for example, through universal Individual Retirement Accounts (IRAs). The Tax Reform Act of 1986 scaled back IRAs, both because the program had a significant revenue cost and because the decline in private saving in the early 1980s coincided with the introduction of IRAs, leading to claims that these incentives were ineffective. In fact, the IRA experience was probably too short to permit a conclusive estimate of how these programs affected saving. While many households will respond to a new saving incentive program by transferring existing assets into tax-deferred accounts, the central question is whether such transfers persist forever and when these accounts begin to encourage new saving.

Several studies suggest that despite the opportunity for asset transfers, most contributions to IRAs constituted new saving or reduced tax payments.[23] More important, the net financial wealth of most U.S. households is relatively low, with median holdings of less than $10,000 even at reasonably high income levels. It is difficult for such households to make sustained transfers into an IRA; in only a few years the median household will exhaust its financial holdings and therefore be required to reduce consumption in order to continue making IRA contributions.[24]

Despite these reasons for optimism about the long-run effects of IRAs on saving, in the short run these programs have an important disadvantage: they reduce federal revenues and exacerbate the deficit. On political grounds, experimenting with nondeductible IRAs with other benefits—for example, tax-exemption for the accrued interest when the funds are withdrawn—may be warranted.

Private saving consists of both personal and corporate saving, and most policy discussions focus on options for raising the former. In part, this is because the principal policies to raise business saving involve either reduced corporate taxes, which exacerbate the deficit and have little current support, or higher taxes on corporate dividend distributions to reduce payout and therefore encourage firms to retain earnings. The second class of policies, precisely contrary to prevailing political winds toward integration of the personal and corporate tax systems, would adversely affect the cost of capital.

One policy that affects corporate behavior and would raise private saving is equalizing the tax treatment of debt and equity. During the 1980s, corporate share repurchases became an important device for transferring cash from firms to their shareholders. A substantial fraction of these repurchases was financed by corporate borrowing, in part because tax reforms during the 1980s made debt more attractive than equity finance and provided an incentive for firms to replace equity with debt in their capital structures.

The tax incentives for debt finance depend on taxes on investors as well as corporations. During the past decade, reductions in the top marginal tax rate on interest income (from 70 percent in 1980 to 50 percent in 1981 to 28 percent in 1986) reduced the tax burden on corporate borrowing and increased the attractiveness of corporate debt for individual investors. In 1980, a top-bracket individual received $0.30 in after-tax interest payments if a corporation earned $1.00 and paid this dollar as interest, compared with $0.31 if he held corporate equity.[25] In 1989, the analogous after-tax incomes are $0.72 for debt and $0.52 for equity. The after-tax return from holding debt has increased faster than that from holding equity, prompting changes in corporate capital structure.

The disparity between debt and equity taxation artificially encourages corporate borrowing, and it also encourages debt-for-equity swaps, which may reduce private saving by encouraging consumption of accrued but previously unrealized capital gains.[26] A revenue-neutral reform which equalized the tax burdens on debt and equity, for example, by making dividend payments tax deductible and raising the statutory corporate tax rate to make up revenue losses, would therefore encourage private saving.

Raising Government Saving. Although raising private saving would raise national saving, none of the options described above is certain to make an immediate and substantial impact on the national saving rate. In contrast, increased government saving—deficit reduction—would probably have such an effect. There is unfortunately little agreement on the appropriate method for tightening fiscal policy. This section begins by discussing options for spending cuts, and then considers a variety of revenue raisers. Each of these options involves tradeoffs, and there is no policy option that will appeal to all interest groups. Nevertheless, it is possible to sketch the menu for potential action.

Spending reduction. Significant spending cuts were enacted in the late 1980s, although they have been insufficient to stem the deficit's growth. As a share of GNP, discretionary domestic federal spending has been rolled back to its level in the early 1960s, and further reductions seem likely. Real defense spending has declined more than 5 percent since its peak in 1987, and nondefense discretionary spending as a share of GNP has declined from 5.8 percent in 1980 to less than 4 percent at present.

Table 1–16 shows the effect of several mechanical policies for slowing spending growth. Table 1–16 focuses on either one-year freezes in program outlays at 1989 levels, or on strategies for reducing

37

TABLE 1–16
DEFICIT REDUCTION EFFECTS OF SPENDING CUTS, FISCAL
YEARS 1990–1994
(nominal current dollars, billions)

Policy Action	1990	1991	1992	1993	1994
Eliminate COLA adjustments for non-means-tested benefits, 1989	10.6	14.6	14.8	14.8	14.7
Discretionary nondefense outlays					
One-year program freeze	2.9	4.9	5.8	6.2	6.6
Program freeze at 1989 spending levels	2.9	8.0	14.0	20.3	27.1
Restriction to 2% annual growth	1.5	4.2	5.8	6.2	6.6
Defense outlays					
Freeze defense program levels and pay (1989 levels)	5.9	15.7	27.0	39.0	51.7
2% annual increase in program levels and pay	3.0	8.3	14.4	20.8	27.8
One-year (1989) program and pay freeze	5.9	9.4	11.0	11.8	12.6

SOURCE: Congressional Budget Office, *Reducing the Deficit: Spending and Revenue Options*, Washington, D.C., February 1989.

prospective program growth. Given the growth and importance of transfers in the current federal budget, the first row considers omitting cost-of-living increases in non-means-tested benefits (such as social security) for 1989. This would save nearly $15 billion per year during 1991–1994, while distributing the burden relatively evenly across transfer recipients.[27] The rationale for such a program is that transfers have expanded rapidly during the past two decades. Since 1970, for example, real social security benefits have grown 1 percent per year faster than wages. Forgoing the cost of living increase would bring the transfer growth patterns into closer alignment with other income flows.

The relative magnitude of different spending programs is illustrated by the next two rows in table 1–16, which consider freezing discretionary nondefense outlays. This category excludes the majority of transfer programs, and yields relatively small deficit-reduction benefits.

Table 1–16 also shows the deficit reduction from various reductions in defense outlays. Since defense outlays are substantially larger than nondefense discretionary spending, applying similar spending limitations to defense yields larger outlay reductions.

One reason for considering mechanical spending cuts, such as program freezes, is that these policies are similar to the deficit-reduction strategies which enforce the current deficit targets. The Balanced Budget and Emergency Deficit Control Act, which Congress passed in 1985 and reaffirmed in 1987, sets target levels for the total deficit, measured as the sum of on- and off-budget deficits. These targets are enforced through across-the-board spending reductions (half from defense, half from nondefense outlays) whenever the targets are exceeded by more than $10 billion. These measures are frequently viewed as a painful way to reduce the deficit because the prescribed reductions in nondefense outlays would involve large program cuts. Congress could avoid this procedure by agreeing in advance to broader-based expenditure cuts of the type described in table 1–16.

Revenue Raising. The political difficulty in generating support for sizable spending cuts, coupled with (a) the need for new revenues to support spending on emerging priorities like education, infrastructure, and civilian research and development and (b) the need to restore tax incentives to spur saving and investment, makes a tax increase in the next few years almost inevitable. Satisfying the deficit-reduction targets in the 1987 Act, which calls for *no deficit* in 1992, will be particularly difficult without new taxes. Two broad approaches are possible—broad-based taxes that raise revenue with minimal effects on economic incentives, and piecemeal reforms that raise taxes on particular activities viewed as socially harmful or that introduce incremental increases in traditional revenue instruments. Given the rhetoric of the 1988 presidential campaign, there may be a premium on raising revenue without changing tax rates. There are many ways to do this: repealing income tax indexing would raise revenues, even though such a change would not be perceived as a "tax increase" by many.

The political climate suggests that major new revenue initiatives are unlikely to receive enough support to be viable during the early 1990s. The value-added tax, for example, while imposing relatively low tax rates and therefore minimizing distortions in economic activity, is perceived as a "money machine" by many and therefore is not likely to be politically viable.

Table 1–17 presents several options for increasing revenues. Although in isolation many of the options have small effects on the deficit, combining several instruments could lead to substantial increases in government saving. Pursuing the earlier argument that transfer programs, particularly social security, could be pared to

39

TABLE 1–17
DEFICIT REDUCTION EFFECTS OF REVENUE RAISERS, FISCAL
YEARS 1990–1994
(nominal current dollars, billions)

Policy Action	1990	1991	1992	1993	1994
Income tax reforms					
Tax 50% of employer-contributed social security benefits (no thresholds)	2.4	8.2	8.7	9.4	10.1
Cap mortgage interest tax deduction at 15%	3.6	10.0	10.9	11.8	12.8
Tax some employer-paid health insurance (> $250/ month)	4.7	8.6	11.4	15.3	20.5
Enact 5% surtax	12.6	24.0	26.0	28.2	30.6
Extend 33% top bracket	3.6	5.1	8.7	10.4	15.1
Raise marginal rates to 16% and 30%	17.3	32.9	35.7	38.8	42.0
Eliminate state-local tax deductibility	4.1	27.9	29.6	31.4	33.3
Eliminate capital gains basis step-up at death	0.3	5.5	5.5	5.5	5.4
Other options					
5% corporate income surtax	3.4	6.0	6.3	6.5	6.9
Increase motor fuel excise by 12 cents per gallon	11.9	11.5	11.4	11.4	11.6
Raise cigarette tax by 16 cents per pack	2.9	2.9	2.9	2.8	2.7
Increase excises on beer and wine to distilled spirit rate	4.7	4.8	4.9	4.9	5.0
Value-added tax (5%)					
On comprehensive base	0.0	82.3	125.4	136.4	147.5
Excluding food, medical, and housing expenditures	0.0	47.3	72.0	78.3	84.3

SOURCE: Congressional Budget Office, *Reducing the Deficit: Spending and Revenue Options*, Washington, D.C., February 1989.

reduce the deficit, the first option considers changes in the tax treatment of social security benefits. One option is to tax the portion of social security benefits that do not represent the return of workers' contributions.

Other options for broadening the base of income tax include capping mortgage interest deductions by allowing such deductions at a 15 percent tax rate, and taxing employer-provided health insurance, which might have salutary effects in slowing the growth of outlays on medical care and would move the tax system toward more accurate taxation of true economic income.

Table 1–17 also identifies several tax options that constitute "new taxes" but might warrant consideration.

Another revenue option, not shown in table 1–17, is tightening the enforcement of existing tax laws. While the precise revenue yield from increased enforcement is uncertain, approximately $100 billion of potential revenue is lost each year because of tax evasion. There is little doubt that increases in the Internal Revenue Service budget are repaid several times over with increased revenues. The audit rate today is substantially lower than it was two decades ago, making it unlikely that a return to previous levels would be viewed as an important invasion of privacy or considered an unacceptable government intrusion into the lives of taxpayers.

The final two rows in table 1–17 illustrate the revenue potential of a value-added tax (VAT). A 5 percent national sales tax on a comprehensive base could raise nearly $150 billion per year by 1994, making this the only revenue option under consideration that in isolation could close the current federal deficit and would even offer some promise for bringing the on-budget accounts to near balance.

Redefining the Deficit: Proposals for Budgetary Reform. The federal budget process is currently anchored by the deficit reduction targets in the Balanced Budget Act. Why should a current Congress be bound by the limits suggested by previous Congresses? In practice the targets have two important functions:

First, they provide a benchmark for budget deliberations, an objective standard against which the president's budget proposal or congressional modifications can be evaluated. Media discussions of whether particular proposals meet the deficit targets may encourage frugality by both the president and the legislature.

Second, the sequestration procedures through which cutbacks occur enable current legislators to shirk some responsibility for spending reductions, blaming the cuts on the previous Congress that enacted the budget targets. If Congress and the president cannot agree on a set of cutbacks, the bill provides for a default deficit reduction strategy. If this is not too painful—imposing particularly harsh cutbacks in some areas—it may be allowed to take effect. Alternatively, if the sequestration plans are perceived as inequitable or especially burdensome, the threat of their effect provides a motive for budgetary compromise.

Discussions of budget targets inevitably lead to proposals for a balanced budget amendment. While this would bind future legislatures even more than the current budgetary targets, it goes too far. There are circumstances when government deficits are necessary components of expansionary government policy, and the requirement of a balanced budget would make it impossible for Congress and the president to use fiscal policy toward this end.

Concluding Remarks

In the 1980s U.S. spending exceeded income, external assets declined and turned negative, and investment was depressed relative to previous decades. There is no assurance that living standards will continue growing at the rate they have in the past. The adjustment in the budget which we argue is essential will not be easy: in fact, it is bound to make the real income squeeze of the 1980s even more acute. But that medicine is far preferable to letting things drift further, with investment low or dependent on foreign saving and the U.S. position in world competition eroding further.

Record low saving and investment, rising external debt, high real interest rates, and an overly strong dollar are the symptoms of an economy that is misaligned. In the 1980s deficits played a useful role in bringing the economy to full employment; that role has now been completed. Now we are facing the challenge of making wise decisions at full employment where the transition to a growth-oriented policy requires higher saving, both private and public.

Expansionary fiscal policy, coupled with tight money in the early 1980s, was among the principal factors in raising U.S. interest rates in the 1980s above historical levels and in causing dollar appreciation on an unprecedented scale. Adjustments in the budget can now help reverse that unproductive policy constellation. With budget cutting we can expect a reversal of the 1980s crowding-out; tighter fiscal policy would be accompanied by an easing of money so that the U.S. economy can be assured of full employment. Lower interest rates would stimulate investment but would also help bring down the dollar and thus raise net exports. Foreign borrowing would decline as the United States stops building up debts and starts earning its way in the world economy. There is no urgency in completing this process, but it is essential to get it under way.

2

Tax Policy in the 1990s

C. Eugene Steuerle

Tax policy in the 1990s will be guided only partly by traditional considerations in tax policy. Tax legislation since the enactment of the Tax Reform Act of 1986 already shows the handwriting on the wall. Two of the most significant tax changes in 1988 and 1989 were (1) increases in taxes (or fees) on savers to help finance the bailout of thrift institutions and (2) adoption—and elimination—of a surtax on the elderly to pay for an expansion of Medicare. Even before tax reform, Congress had begun to enact sometimes small, sometimes moderate deficit-reduction packages that contained tax increases. Most of these were driven by budget considerations or, as in the 1983 social security reform, by concern with the total structure, not just the tax component, of a system of government.

Financing considerations have often been given only secondary attention when various domestic programs were expanded or reformed. In the 1990s the pattern will reverse itself, and financing considerations will become dominant. The future is foretold in part by recent events, such as the presidential and congressional mandates on the Treasury Department, not the Department of Health and Human Services, to direct a major study on financing health care.[1] In sum the financing side of many expenditure issues will drive much tax policy. Broad reforms of such governmental systems as health, social security, welfare, and regulation of the environment will further break down the somewhat arbitrary division of public finance issues into expenditure, tax, and budget components. The legislative trend toward treating expenditure and tax changes simultaneously will accelerate.

More traditional tax issues will not go away. The past trend toward taxing workers more and more each decade may finally come to an end and could even reverse itself. Tax simplification is a logical

---

Some discussions are taken from the author's "Economic Perspectives" column in *Tax Notes*. Reprinted by permission.

follow-up to any period of major reform, and there are a number of impetuses to act on this front. The rapid evolution of financial markets, both at home and abroad, forces consideration of how to tax equity relative to debt (and whether to integrate corporate and personal income taxes) and how to treat capital income in an international setting where financial assets can be transferred abroad almost instantaneously. Saving and investment incentives are proposed on a perennial basis and will not go away. Finally, I foresee renewal of a debate on the role of fiscal policy in a recession, even though deficits in the early 1990s may prevent much additional countercyclical policy.

All in all, the message is a mixed one. In domestic policy our government remains in a long period of stalemate, where movement to tackle new problems is prevented by an unwillingness to provide the resources necessary to do so. Because these resources can be provided both by other expenditure decreases and by tax increases, one would be mistaken to believe that the symbolic debate of expenditures versus taxes is the main cause of forestalled action. Instead the political process encourages cowardice toward admitting that any shift in priorities requires resources and sacrifices from some part of the public.

From an economic standpoint the connection of financing and expenditure decisions is often appropriate. An ideal budget process would consider all trade-offs at the same time so that the benefits and costs of each additional action can be compared with other alternatives and opportunities. Our political process unfortunately has yet to discover how to engage efficiently in this type of process. As a result there is inaction on many fronts. Even when worthwhile expenditure changes are made on one side of the budget, they are often offset by poor tax policy on the other side of the budget—or vice versa. Finally, we only tackle well-recognized problems when they reach crisis proportion or are made into popular issues by the media. The failures of the Federal Savings and Loan Insurance Corporation (FSLIC) and the Department of Housing and Urban Development (HUD) are two examples of this type of policy making—and of the high cost entailed in delaying necessary action for years.

A Brief History

The current period of government muddling cannot be understood without a broader historical perspective of events that have led us here. An unavoidable balance sheet requirement is imposed on all decisions on tax and expenditure. Any expansion of an expenditure program, for instance, necessarily implies higher taxes, greater deficits, and higher future taxes, or reductions in other expenditure programs. The current stalemate can best be understood in terms of those balances: we can no longer use the old ways of achieving balance and of adapting government efforts to current needs. New ways have yet to be found.

After World War II, balances were provided in four principal ways. First, especially in the early postwar era, there was a large and unexpected inflation tax on the outstanding stock of debt. Deficits in effect could be financed partially by declines in the real value of a large outstanding stock of debt. Because the acceleration of inflation was partially unexpected, moreover, interest rates on the debt tended to be low in real terms. Second, there was a significant decline in the defense budget relative to gross national product (GNP), with exceptions for the Korean and Vietnam wars and for the slight build-up in the 1980s. Third, there was bracket creep in the individual income tax—in particular, bracket creep brought about by inflation. Fourth, there were continual and little-debated increases in social security tax rates, often enacted because of a requirement to keep the trust funds solvent. The evolution of social security taxation was so steady that it can be traced by a simple rule of thumb: three percentage points per decade. At the end of every decade the combined social security tax rate has increased almost exactly three percentage points, reaching 3.0 percent in 1950; 6.0 percent in 1960; 9.6 percent in 1970; 12.26 percent in 1980; and 15.3 percent in 1990. These social security tax increases were by far the major source of financing changes in domestic policy during the last half-century.

Until the 1980s these four sources of revenues did not simply pay for expansions in domestic expenditures. They paid for a variety of changes in tax policy as well. Debates about tax reductions paralleled debates on expansion of expenditures such as Medicare and social security. Also accompanying each tax reduction was a series of tax provisions designed to provide new sources of subsidy or expenditure through the tax code. While a tax bill might temporarily reduce revenues, over a several-year period it was paid for by the four major sources of revenue. In effect revenues did not go down at all but remained rather constant. From 1960 to 1990, a period with a significant amount of tax legislation, receipts were never less than 17.4 percent of GNP (in 1965) nor more than 20.1 percent of GNP (in 1969 and 1981); they are currently just over 19 percent of GNP.

As the nation moved into the late 1970s and the 1980s, all of these sources of revenues for expenditure or tax changes were reduced in importance or eliminated. First, the stock of debt relative to GNP declined significantly until the late 1970s and thus reduced any real decline that might be due to inflation. Interest rates also rose well in excess of the rate of inflation. Second, defense expenditures declined in importance relative to GNP and made declines in defense a less important source of revenues. Third, bracket creep in the individual income tax has been reduced greatly because of indexation for inflation. Finally, and most important, for the first time in five decades the social security system is due for a period with no increase in tax rates. Between 1990 and 2000 we are unlikely to see the traditional increase in tax rates of three percentage points per decade.

This story is somewhat simplified. Recent inflation rates of 4 and 5 percent are actually serving again as a means to help reduce the real value of the outstanding stock of debt and hence to offset increases in debt due to deficits. A so-called peace dividend is already being spent at a fairly fast rate to finance other changes in the budget, although this dividend is small relative to those available after World War II, Korea, and Vietnam.[2] Some believe that a social security tax increase will be necessary eventually to finance the retirement of the baby-boom generation. Thus, there certainly can be periods during which one or another of these four sources of revenues might be made available temporarily. Regardless of possible periodic changes, however, these four sources of revenue are no longer available on a regular basis; they are not automatic, nor, relative to the size of the economy, are they likely to be as important as in the past.

During the 1970s our institutions were not yet ready for the changes about to be forced upon them. When President Carter asked the Department of Health and Human Services for a deficit-neutral welfare reform bill, for instance, he was rebuffed by Congress and his own appointees. Only a decade later, in 1988, was welfare reform required to be almost deficit-neutral by making simultaneous changes in other tax and expenditure provisions.

In the 1980s President Reagan did establish a new set of priorities: to reduce taxes and to increase defense expenditures. Congress balked at paying for these shifts in priorities by reducing other expenditures, while the president balked at increasing taxes. With the adoption of indexing of tax brackets in 1981 (effective in 1984), and with the last social security tax increase scheduled for 1990, however, no one can rely upon the old sources of funds to pay for new priorities.

The implications were evident in legislation enacted throughout the 1980s. In 1984 through 1986, for instance, it was obvious that the old method of paying for a tax reform through a revenue-losing bill— a method that never worked—was no longer available. Every reduction in the tax rate or increase in personal exemption had to be paid for through a reduction or elimination of some special preference or deduction. Under one calculation tax reform achieved the equivalent of a reduction in expenditures of close to $190 billion per year.[3]

Future Dominance of Financing Issues

Many believe that the current debate on the budget deficit prevents major changes in policy: once the deficit is eliminated, policy choices will be easier. This is incorrect. The debate over the deficit is mainly a debate over how to provide sources of expenditure reduction or tax increase to pay for an increase in national, or at least federal, saving. Once that saving is achieved—only one of many possible new priorities—the same dispute will be with us. Any other change in priorities also will require expenditure reduction or tax increase and cannot be financed as changes were throughout most of the postwar era.

The 1990s will see a further evolution of institutions to accommodate this new reality. Although a peace dividend and the retirement of a relatively small generation of individuals (the baby-bust population of the era of the depression and World War II) provide some reprieve in the short run, neither really solves the long-run issue of how new resources will be provided.

As a result the tax policy of the 1990s will be guided in large part by the vicissitudes and evolution of this budget and expenditure process. Given the enactment of tax reform in 1986, I see no effort at major tax reform in the near future, although many tax issues will still be addressed. The one caveat, an important one, is that major tax changes usually result from major crises such as recession or failing institutions. Although some crises are almost inevitable, I do not want to speculate loosely here on what they might be or what fiscal reactions they will call forth.

Even if we are so lucky as to avoid the types of crises that often lead to major changes in tax policy, the congressional tax-writing committees will remain extraordinarily busy. Again history gives us a guide. Few may think of the 1987 deficit reduction as involving significant changes in taxation, but a member of the House Ways and Means Committee correctly argued that 80 percent of the deficit-reducing decisions were being made in that committee rather than in other committees in the House.

Few seem to understand why so much policy concerning labor, family, welfare, and other expenditure falls within the bailiwick of the tax writers. Yet one source of power should be obvious: they control the entire revenue side of the budget. Every dollar that is spent is paid for through taxes now or taxes later. In addition about one-third of nondefense expenditures and subsidies fall into the tax code. The housing budget of the Department of Housing and Urban Development, for example, is dwarfed in importance by the housing provisions in the tax code. Or the business provisions under the purview of the Commerce Department can be compared with those business decisions affected by the tax code.

With any major expenditure or tax change of the last decade or so, the tax-writing committees were usually a major, and often the dominant, participant. Excluding tax reform, these actions include much of the deficit reduction in 1982, 1984, and 1987; social security reform in 1983; catastrophic health insurance in 1988 and 1989; and welfare reform in 1988.

A related reason for the power of the tax-writing committees is the breadth of their responsibility. They have enough issues within their jurisdiction that they often can make a significant change in almost any domestic policy—housing, education, welfare, and so forth—simply by putting the change in the tax code, coming up with the necessary resources through other tax changes, and thereby avoiding a need for support from any other committee. No expenditure, budget, or appropriations committee has a similar ability to make trade-offs.

Thus, while tax reform itself is not expected on the near-term agenda, tax policy will remain extraordinarily active. The financing side of policy issues will continue to dominate the decision-making process, and many budget and expenditure issues will be handled through the tax code. For at least the early 1990s, most major policy decisions will be made by the tax-writing committees, the only ones that are capable of dealing with the balance sheet and trade-off aspects of most issues with which they deal.

Likely Tax Issues of the 1990s

For the following tax issues, the probability of action is at least significant, and in a few cases likely, in the 1990s. These issues are arbitrarily divided into three groups: traditional tax issues, tax issues driven by concerns over the deficit, and tax changes likely to accompany structural reform of other governmental systems such as social security and welfare (see table 2–1). In many cases there is much overlap. Expansion of the tax base to cover untaxed income, for instance, may be justified on traditional tax policy grounds of tax equity or efficiency as a means to reduce the deficit and increase federal saving or as a way to reallocate resources within a government system of expenditure, regulation, and taxation.

Traditional Tax Issues. We will examine six issues.

The taxation of workers. Considerable attention may soon be paid to the ways in which workers are taxed under both social security

TABLE 2–1

A MENU OF TAX ISSUES FOR THE 1990s

Traditional Tax Issues
- Taxation of workers
  Historic trend toward increased taxes dampened, if not reversed.
- Tax simplification
  Logical follow-up to a period of rapid change and reform.
- International tax issues
  Inevitable result of an increasingly interdependent world with mobile financial capital.
- Integration of corporate and individual income taxes
  Reincarnation due to backdoor integration, complex and inconsistent rules for corporate transactions, and international comparisons.
- More saving and investment incentives
  A perennial offering of popular, yet ineffectual, sops.
- Fiscal policy for a recession
  Renewal of an old, almost forgotten, debate.

Deficit-Reduction Tax Issues
- Flexible freeze or limited growth of tax expenditures
  Logical corollary to limited growth of direct expenditures.
- Increase in excise taxes
  Merely a restoration of excises at well below historically high levels.

Structural Reform of Other Governmental Systems
- Reform of social security tax
  Momentum led by concern for taxes paid by workers, long-term problems of the social security and Medicare systems, and existing discrimination against women, secondary workers, and some minorities.
- Reform in health and Medicare
  Financing concerns predominant for the major domestic policy issue of the 1990s.
- Reform of transfer and welfare
  Taxation of benefits as a partial way to integrate diverse tax and transfer schemes, to devote a greater share of resources to the long-term and working poor, and to provide revenues for other welfare reforms.
- Reform of other regulatory and insurance systems

(Table continues on next page.)

TABLE 2–1 (continued)

Tax changes to accompany redesign of government systems that provide insurance for saving deposits, insurance against the unfunded liabilities of private pension plans, and regulation and control of environmental waste and pollution.

Reactions to Crises
• Any or all of the above, plus more
  Congressional chefs guaranteed to mix up an interesting stew, with tax writers supplying many ingredients.

and income tax, long an issue of little concern. The focus of the debate on tax policy for several decades has been how or whether to reduce taxes on capital income and how to raise revenues to pay for expansion of social welfare programs, in particular, social security. Since the residual always gets squeezed, it is not surprising that most major expenditure increases and tax decreases of the past few decades have been paid for by increases in taxes on workers.

Let us take the case of moderate income workers who still earn considerably less than median income in the economy. As table 2–2 suggests, the direct tax burden of a family at one-half the median income has gone up considerably, from almost nothing in 1948 to about one-fifth of income by 1990.[4]

TABLE 2–2

TAX RATES FOR FOUR-PERSON FAMILIES AT ONE-HALF THE MEDIAN INCOME, 1948–1990

(percent)

Year	Average Income Tax Rate	Social Security Tax Rate
1948	0.00	2.00
1954	0.00	4.00
1960	0.15	6.00
1966	2.72	8.40
1972	4.37	10.40
1978	4.73	12.10
1984	6.50	13.40
1990	5.57	15.30

SOURCE: Eugene Steuerle and Paul Wilson, "The Taxation of Poor and Lower Income Workers," in Ladders out of Poverty: A Report of the Project on the Welfare of Families, edited by Jack A. Meyer (Washington, D.C.: American Horizons Foundation, 1986), and data furnished by Al Lerman, U.S. Treasury.

Although the evidence has been extraordinarily weak, many policy makers have adopted a conventional view that taxes on workers do not cause much change in behavior, whereas taxes on saving cause distortions that need to be addressed.[5] In addition, labor income is so large relative to total income in society that even modest increases on the tax rate on labor can raise significant sums of money when needed. As a corollary, modest tax reductions for workers run into the double bind that they will not appear to do a great deal on a per-capita basis but will have a significant effect on the budget deficit. It is far better for a politician to give larger sums of money to much smaller groups of people and hence to maintain at least the appearance of doing more. That is one reason why tax breaks to savers or investors are so popular even when economically ineffective. The year 1990 will give a perfect example of this type of logic. Congress and the executive branch will debate giving away a few billion dollars in the form of a saving incentive even while they allow a social security tax increase to raise taxes on workers by a multiple of what they will give away.

Concerns about equity, rather than efficiency, will drive the consideration of tax rates on labor in the 1990s. We can consider the changes since 1960, when the top individual rate for income tax was 90 percent—more than fifteen times the social security tax rate. The top individual rate has fallen to less than twice the social security tax rate.

Today almost two of three taxpayers pay more in combined employee plus employer social security tax than they do in federal income tax. For most workers the combined social security and income tax rates are as high as or higher than the top rates paid by the highest-income individuals in society. Thus for most workers in the 15 percent income tax bracket and many in the 28 percent income tax bracket, an additional 15.3 percent of earnings paid in the form of social security tax moves them above or well above the tax rate paid by the highest-income taxpayers, who pay only an income tax rate of 28 percent.[6]

If we then start to take into account other differences, the comparison becomes even more dramatic. If we consider those workers who are in the phase-out range of the earned-income tax credit—which phases out currently at a 10 percent rate—each additional dollar of earnings causes an increase in tax (counting reduction of credit) of close to forty cents. If we take into account costs of child care and commuting, then the net marginal returns for earning an additional dollar may fall to thirty cents, fifteen cents, or even zero for some individuals.

We can go beyond the direct tax system and add in those who are eligible for welfare payments, as well as those who have moved just beyond eligibility for benefits. The phase-out of income transfers and food stamps, as well as the elimination of Medicaid benefits, places extraordinarily high tax rates on many individuals. Tax rates at some income levels, combined with costs of working, can easily exceed 100 percent.

Of special concern here might be the way in which taxes are increased and transfer payments are reduced when a single male marries a low-income single female with children. A number of recent efforts have linked earnings trends to declining marriage rates and the growth of female-headed households.[7] Concern over these trends is likely to lead to some focus on the large marriage penalties implicit in the combined tax and transfer system.

Tax simplification. Tax simplification has always been on the list of difficult reforms that should be supported—but at some distant point in the future. Now is the time for tax simplification. Simplification is a natural follow-up to any major governmental reform such as the Tax Reform Act of 1986.

The type of simplification called for is one that is consistent with the basic goals of the 1986 reform. Hence drastic simplifications that involve considerable changes in progressivity now are inappropriate. Flat rate taxes, for instance, might allow significant simplification by providing for withholding at the source and no reporting on the part of the taxpayer. But they also require abandonment of the progressivity of the income tax.

The simplifications that should be sought now would result from sifting through the tax code provision by provision and asking whether there are simpler or more direct ways of achieving the implicit goals of each. Where provisions are extraordinarily cumbersome, involve high rates of error or noncompliance, or are simply window dressing, strong consideration should be given to their repeal or reform.

Examples are not hard to find. The additional depreciation schedule for the minimum tax raises little revenue relative to its burden on taxpayers. The elimination of the personal exemption for dependent taxpayers has probably put many of our youth in noncompliance with the law. The claim of exemptions for dependent parents has an extraordinarily high error rate. The annual report for sole proprietors with Keogh plans is needlessly complicated. Tax laws related to fringe benefits have become extraordinarily complex and have raised costs too much for small employers.

One procedure that should be adopted is to let the data guide some efforts toward simplification. I have proposed, for instance, that information on underreporting by type of income and overreporting by type of deduction be used as one guide for provisions that need reform. When error rates exceed 15 percent, for instance, we ought to conclude almost automatically that a change is needed.

One source of pressure for simplification comes from tax practitioners in the legal and accounting professions. Many claim privately that they simply cannot understand and comply with all of the provisions in the law. Instead they guess and subject themselves to the audit lottery. The difficulty with this practice is that it works against one of the basic underpinnings of the U.S. tax system: the reliance upon the abilities and integrity of professional tax preparers to get it right the first time.

International tax issues. For several reasons international tax issues will become one of the more active areas for tax policy in the 1990s. First, some of the changes enacted in 1986 are so complex that few practitioners understand what is required. At a minimum some attempts will be made to make rules workable. Second, the growing interdependence of the economies of different countries and the ease with which financial capital can be transferred across boundaries force renewed consideration of how taxes on multinational businesses should be assessed. Third, the capital flight from third world countries and the hiding of assets in safe havens make the need for cooperation and the development of consistent tax laws imperative. Finally, the old consensus that real corporate capital should be taxed at the source, while individual receipts of interest and dividends should be taxed at the residence, has always produced a schizophrenic result. In a world where financial capital flows freely and forms of debt can easily replace equity, the result may also prove unstable.

While international tax issues will be almost unavoidable in the 1990s, no firm consensus will develop by the end of the decade for what should be done. Some simplification and greater cooperation through tax treaties for exchange of information seem to be the surest routes for positive improvement. Nonetheless the debate will extend far beyond these two approaches to taxation in an international setting.

Integration of corporate and individual income taxes. Another capital income issue will not go away in the 1990s despite the difficulty in passing any such legislation in the United States. The double taxation of corporate income continues to create disparities in taxation between corporate and noncorporate capital and between debt and equity. Corporate integration has been proposed by both the Carter and Reagan administrations.

Several events or considerations are likely to reawaken interest among policy makers in the integration of corporate and individual income taxes: future increases in the debt of the corporate sector; indirect integration achieved by the formation of new businesses in partnership form; and the prejudice in the current tax system against new, risky ventures that must be formed as corporations. The corporate debt issue has been highlighted recently in hearings on leveraged buyouts (LBOs). While there is evidence that corporate debt has increased because of such LBO activity, the corporate sector actually has shown a modest growth rate in debt over the postwar era relative to households and noncorporate businesses.[8] In addition, simply enacting anti-LBO legislation may merely shift, rather than decrease, the amount of borrowing.

Regardless of LBO activity, the corporate sector is likely to increase its share of total debt. The dramatic expansion of noncorporate debt, encouraged in part by favorable tax and regulatory treatment of savings and loans, soon may be over. If this source of demand is reduced in relative terms, corporations may start to outbid households and noncorporate businesses for a larger share of funds that become available for lending. In addition, the Tax Reform Act of 1986 made the corporate tax rate higher than all individual rates. Because deductions are worth most to the highest-rate taxpayer—largely because the real interest rate is overstated by the inflation rate—the corporate sector only recently became the ideal debtor from a tax standpoint, in a reversal of pre-1987 roles.

As the corporate sector increases its debt, it may continue to reduce the relative amount of its equity. In effect, backdoor integration (avoidance of a double tax) is possible for many firms, especially those not engaged in more risky ventures. Such backdoor integration can also be achieved through expansion of the partnership sector relative to the corporate sector. Today many tax advisers argue that new businesses should be set up in partnerships, rather than in a corporate form. Over a long period, these advisers could succeed in further integrating the tax system.

As noted, the extent to which the corporate sector becomes integrated through these mechanisms is often exaggerated. Nonetheless there is a likelihood that Congress will be tempted to step in to channel this integration activity more directly. Some of those actions may move in the opposite direction by defining more clearly what income is subject to additional corporate tax.

More saving and investment incentives. Debates over how to tax capital income are perennial, and they will not go away in the 1990s. Proposals will continue to provide investment and saving incentives, capital gains tax reductions, and special treatment of different types of savings accounts. Over the near term, however, neither Congress nor the administration will be willing to spend much on these items. Therefore, any legislation is likely to represent more sops than substance.

For saving incentives to be effective, they must meet three criteria: (1) they must prevent tax saving simply through asset shifting, (2) they should apply at the margin, and (3) they must not allow individuals to arbitrage the system by borrowing the amount put aside for special tax treatment and at the same time deducting the interest payments.[9] No saving proposal on the table meets these criteria. Only rate reduction so far has managed to meet all of the criteria for a saving incentive.

Even if tax-related saving incentives were effective in inducing some amount of private saving, most actually decrease net national saving because they increase federal dissaving—that is, increase the deficit—more than any rise in private saving. The best forms of saving incentives therefore appear to be reductions in the size of the deficit. (Even this route has no guarantee of success. Increased federal saving [decreased federal deficits] can be absorbed by increased borrowing for consumption by the private sector.)

One failing of the current tax system continually forces capital income tax issues back on the table. The U.S. tax system fails to index for inflation, with several important consequences.[10] First, owners of farmland and real estate, as well as corporate stock, can be subject to significant amounts of taxation on their assets even when no real income has been earned. This factor makes it especially difficult to avoid some form of change in the treatment of capital gains. Second, in times of high inflation, equity ownership of depreciable capital can be heavily taxed. Finally, interest income and expense become among the worst measured of all items of income. A person paying 10 percent interest in a world with 5 percent inflation is deducting twice the real amount of interest expense. Because borrowers and lenders are in different tax brackets, this last factor encourages shifts of hundreds of billions, if not trillions, of dollars of assets among owners. It induces tax shelters to minimize taxes and, when inflation rates are high, helps lead to stagnation of the economy.[11]

Fiscal policy for a recession. It is highly doubtful that the United States will move through the 1990s without suffering from one or more economic downturns. During every recession or slowdown of the economy in recent history, monetary and fiscal policy were

55

brought into play; whether they were effective is another issue. Fiscal policy usually resulted from three changes: (1) both automatic and discretionary increases in outlays for unemployment compensation or similar benefits; (2) decreases in taxes to provide a stimulus to the economy, whether the underlying apologetics were Keynesian or supply-side in orientation; and (3) the adoption of some types of saving and investment incentives. While each of these three policy changes has come into some disrepute these days, we would be mistaken to believe that the politics of a recession will not require some action, or semblance of action, on the part of the federal government.

The first type of fiscal policy is likely to be among the more popular, in part because it can be made temporary in nature. Discretionary increases in payments sometimes take time to work their way into the economy, however. I have already expressed my disdain for the second route: saving and investment incentives. It would be naïve to suggest that Congress and the administration would not react as they have in almost all previous recessions and call for saving or investment incentives as a means to increase the growth rate (which by definition has stagnated in the recession).

Relating the size of the deficit to the condition of the economy is an issue that has been little analyzed in recent years, and the onset of a recession is as likely to call for decreases in the deficit, as increases. According to the Office of Management and Budget, each one-year 1 percent decline in the growth rate of GNP, combined with a 0.5 percent increase in the unemployment rate, would result by the next fiscal year in decreased revenues at a rate of about $11.5 billion annually, with increases in outlay of $3.5 billion. The net change of $15 billion represents about one quarter of 1 percent of GNP, or one quarter of the net change in GNP.[12]

Whether these automatic stabilizers are of the appropriate size, or should be increased or decreased through discretionary action, will probably not get much attention until the actual onset of a recession. If there is an economic slowdown in the early 1990s, my own preference is a modest countercyclical policy in the short run in exchange for greater deficit reduction in the long run. While the economics are fairly sound, the political feasibility of such a scenario remains in doubt.

Deficit-Reduction Tax Issues. Two issues will be discussed here.

Flexible freeze or limited growth of tax expenditures. Tax expenditures have the same economic effect as direct expenditures. Let us suppose one is charged a tax rate of 50 percent, then given the money back in the form of tax credits for purpose X. Net taxes paid are zero; the amount of total expenditures is zero. The government nonetheless has subsidized program X, and in most cases there will be an increase in the output of X and a decrease in the output of other goods and services. The government also has taken 50 percent of the income generated from work and saving and thus affected the extent to which these factors are supplied. In this example, measuring taxes and expenditures as zero is totally misleading.

Both conservative and liberal principles call for a reduction in governmental interference in the marketplace, where such interference is inefficient or regressive. It is hoped that compromises made on the direct expenditure side of the budget will be decided on the basis of such principles. Accordingly these decisions should not be contradicted by action on the tax side of the budget. Reducing expenditures should require reducing tax expenditures at the same time. Any freeze on direct expenditures should be carried over to tax expenditures.

Tax expenditures are often inferior to direct expenditures because the former are not reviewed annually in the budget and they often are designed in a way that would never be considered if the costs were measured and voted upon as direct expenditures. A proposal to cut tax expenditures, however, does not require agreement with this proposition. Instead the proposal requires only that tax and direct expenditures be given equal consideration in a broad effort to reduce the deficit.

Increase in excise taxes. It seems highly improbable that we will move through the 1990s without increasing excise taxes. The term "increase," however, may be misleading. In the early postwar period federal excise taxes were more than 3 percent of GNP. Because most excise taxes are based on quantity, but not price, excise taxes have eroded as inflation has increased the price of most products (see table 2–3). Legislative tax changes have also eliminated or reduced the importance of some excise taxes. Today excise collections represent only about 0.6 percent of GNP. Simply restoring excise tax collections to previous levels could increase tax collections significantly. If by 1992 all excise taxes were to be increased to their 1972 levels, for instance, excise tax receipts would increase about $50 billion. (The net change in receipts would be smaller. Income tax collections decrease when excise tax collections go up.) Similarly, if by 1992 taxes on liquor were increased to their 1980 levels, there would be a $7.5 billion increase in excise tax receipts.

Many of these excise tax changes will be tied to other budgetary changes. Taxes on liquor or tobacco, for instance, might be used to

TABLE 2–3

EXCISE TAXES AS A PERCENTAGE OF GNP, 1948–1992

Year	Percentage of GNP
1948	3.0
1954	2.7
1960	2.3
1966	1.8
1972	1.3
1978	0.8
1984	1.0[a]
1989	0.7
1990	0.6
1991	0.6
1992	0.5

[a]Temporary boost in the late 1970s and early 1980s due to the windfall profits tax on oil.
SOURCE: U.S. Office of Management and Budget, historical table in *Budget of the United States Government* (Washington, D.C.: Government Printing Office, 1989), pp. 28–29. Future years represent estimates under current law.

help finance the fight against drugs. Some increases in excise taxes might be used to reduce other taxes on low-income workers so that the net tax change is not regressive. Many of the trust fund excise taxes—airport and airway, highways, hazardous substance—will be related directly to the financing of changes in transportation, environmental protection, or other policies. By being tied to some expenditure policy, the amount of excise tax increase acceptable to the public would probably be much larger than if the changes were proposed simply to raise revenues. Even if there is a tie-in to an expenditure program, the net impact on the budget often will be deficit reducing. In some cases the excise increase will be used to pay for existing activity. In other cases the excise tax change will substitute for income tax revenues derived from a growing economy and hence leave those revenues for deficit reduction.

Structural Reform of Other Governmental Systems. Five reforms will be addressed here.

Reform of social security tax. The themes of broadening the tax base and spreading tax burdens more evenly among taxpayers is commonly associated with the reform of income tax. Uneven taxation can cause distortions and inequities in any system. The time has come for reform of the social security tax.

A strong case can be made that two workers with equal income should pay the same amount of social security tax. Under existing social security law, however, individuals with equal incomes can pay social security taxes that differ significantly. A worker with $30,000 in cash wages pays more than $1,200 per year more than a worker with a similar amount of income but receiving $8,000 in nontaxable fringe benefits. Over time the tax differences become quite substantial.

Who are the principal victims of this tax discrimination? They are the individuals or groups who are more likely to receive their income in the form of cash compensation rather than fringe benefits. These include part-time workers, women, and some minorities. In addition, when one worker in a family already receives significant fringe benefits such as health insurance, the secondary worker receives little or no benefit from provision of a similar fringe benefit. In a job with substantial fringe benefits, the secondary worker receives little tax benefit when the fringe benefit is essentially worthless. If the secondary worker switches to a job with payment made in cash, then the tax discrimination remains even if equal pay is received for equal work.

Fringe benefits have slowly eroded the social security tax base. Over the past thirty years the social security tax base has declined 10 percent because of such fringe benefits, while another 10 percent decline is projected over the next forty years under the assumptions often used by social security actuaries. With social security and railroad retirement receipts estimated at more than $365 billion for this fiscal 1990, each 10 percent erosion translates to about $35 billion.

Finally, efficiency considerations argue strongly for capping the exclusion of fringe benefits such as health insurance. These fringe-benefit exclusions encourage inefficient decision making with respect to purchases and have an inflationary effect on the cost of health care. This inflation in turn drives up health care costs for those who are not subsidized by the tax system and have to pay for health care or health insurance with their own money.

These arguments are not new. What I suggest, however, is that the reforms could be tied more directly to reform of the social security system rather than made into an income tax issue as in the past. This reform could be motivated by a number of concerns: lower taxes on workers, the long-run insolvency of social security, the huge annual deficits forecast when the baby-boom population retires, the major problems associated with the financing of Medicare, or discrimination against women, secondary workers, and some minorities.

Reform in health and Medicare. Just beneath the surface of the budgetary debate is one nagging and politically sensitive fact: the continual rise in health and Medicare expenditures is the major source of pressure on the budget. The real rate of growth of federal health expenditures continues to exceed the real rate of growth in the economy by several percentage points.

This trend is unsustainable. If we add federal expenditures, state and local expenditures, and tax subsidies, governments contribute more than $300 billion to health care. The hospital insurance trust fund (HI) remains insolvent over the long run. Medical payments to nonhospital providers were projected recently to rise significantly over the next few years in absence of any countervailing legislation.

At the same time the health system is imbalanced because it favors acute medical needs over long-term care needs associated with chronic illness. It is also imbalanced because it favors those with generous employer health plans over those with less generous plans or no plans at all.

Tax policy will be involved intimately in resolving these issues. In 1988 and 1989, individual medical accounts were proposed by the Department of Health and Human Services and by many in Congress as a way to deal with long-term care. A small tax credit to deal with the uninsured nonelderly was contained in a recent bill passed by the Senate Finance Committee. While their effects would be limited, these proposals demonstrate one way that taxes are likely to be brought into play in dealing with issues of health. Similarly the Treasury report *Financing Health Care for Tomorrow* demonstrates ways that we can merge tax rules regarding pensions with rules related to long-term care. It also points out a way to reform tax benefits for the nonelderly so that a greater portion would apply to those who are now uninsured and who suffer the most discrimination from existing tax policy. (At a minimum the tax treatment of prefunded private long-term care plans must be decided, and tax incentives for employees must be coordinated with any tax benefits extended to those not currently covered by employer plans.)

By the end of the decade, if not before, I also expect a major effort to resolve the long-term insolvency of the hospital insurance portion of Medicare (the portion financed through social security taxes), as well as to bring down further the cost of supplementary medical benefits (Medicare, part B). Some related tax proposals will also be considered. It would not be surprising to see issues such as taxation of social security benefits, or even Medicare benefits, brought up in that context.

Reform of transfer payments and welfare. The 1990s are also likely to see major efforts to restructure the welfare and transfer systems in this country. In the process of restructuring, tax issues are likely to come once again to the fore.

Taxation of benefits will be one area of attention. Benefit taxation, however, will be difficult to enact purely as a means to raise revenues or to improve tax equity. Rather taxation of benefits is likely to be considered as part of a broader package of expenditure and tax reform. This would be consistent with many recent enactments. The taxation of up to one-half of social security benefits, for instance, was made part of a social security package enacted in 1983 that restored the actuarial soundness of the program. The original taxation of unemployment compensation was also part of an effort to increase direct payments during a recession.

Taxing transfer payments would represent another major step toward structuring programs in a more integrated fashion. Taxation would make available in one agency, the Internal Revenue Service, the data necessary to examine the interaction of all the various tax and transfer systems that are often designed with inadequate attention to each other.

Taxation would effectively recoup some benefits when overlapping layers of eligibility result in combined benefit levels that exceed tax-free levels of income. At the same time taxation is based upon an annual accounting period rather than the monthly accounting period common to welfare programs. The longer-term poor therefore would be less likely to pay taxes than those who are poor for only part of a year. If the money from taxation were returned to the income-transfer programs, the shift toward an annual accounting period would likely move a greater share of net benefits toward the longer-term poor.

Taxation of social security benefits is potentially the most significant of possible changes in the taxation of transfer payments. The taxation of such benefits is one of the items that may well be on the table when solutions are sought for the long-term solvency of the social security trust funds, the upcoming retirement of the baby-boom population, or the intermediate-term insolvency of the Medicare hospital insurance trust fund.

Reform of other regulatory and insurance systems. Tax issues at times interact with other government efforts in the economy. We can consider the case of government insurance. Taxes or fees must be collected directly or indirectly when the government acts as insurer. These costs may be assessed against those insured, against those who undertake the risk, or against the public. When the insurance system is improperly designed, significant increases in taxes may be necessary to make the system more fully funded.

The recent FSLIC crisis makes obvious what happens when an

insurance system is designed improperly. New fees are now imposed on financial institutions; those fees result in an increased gap between what borrowers pay and savers receive. Because these fees are insufficient to cover losses, however, significant amounts of government revenues eventually must be supplied from other sources.

Most government insurance systems remain poorly designed. We can therefore expect to see taxes and fees of various sorts proposed to solve crises with savings and loans, banks, and the Pension Benefit Guarantee Corporation. It is hoped that consideration will be given to the actual reform of these systems as well.

Taxes can also be used as alternatives to government systems of regulation. Researchers have long proposed converting environmental regulation to a system of incentives and disincentives. More recently congressional hearings have centered on market- or tax-based approaches to regulation, and President Bush has suggested or considered various forms of taxes to pay for environmental problems.

These tax proposals have a long way to go. Some taxes, for instance, need to be assessed on a geographical basis, yet many tax mechanisms are more universal in their effect. How to measure what is to be taxed remains a difficult problem. Nonetheless a basic appeal remains to assess a tax on the relationship to costs imposed upon society. Not only is greater efficiency achieved, but the distortionary effects of using other taxes to raise revenues can be reduced.

Conclusion

Tax policy will remain a lively arena during the 1990s. Some changes will be forced by a changing economy and environment. Other changes, proposed for years, may finally come to fruition in the 1990s. And some issues simply will never die. Much of tax policy, however, will be guided less by traditional concerns about tax policy than by efforts to reduce the deficit and to achieve structural reform of social security, health, Medicare, welfare, environmental protection, and other systems. The high level of activity proceeds from a system where two-thirds of domestic economic policy flows through the tax code, and tax writers are among the few policy makers who can and often must make trade-offs among a wide range of expenditure and tax functions.

3
Federal Spending Issues of the 1990s

Rudolph G. Penner

A forecaster is happy to predict federal spending issues for the next ten years because it takes a decade to be proved wrong definitively. Almost certainly, such a forecast will be wrong, but the more interesting question is, How wrong is it likely to be?

It should, in fact, be relatively easy to identify the key issues underlying the major trends in civilian spending. At the end of the 1980s, 44 percent of gross nondefense, noninterest spending and about 27 percent of gross total spending was absorbed by only two program categories—old-age, survivors, and disability insurance (OASDI, or social security) and Medicare (see table 3–1). Projections of the elderly and disabled population over the next decade are likely to be highly accurate, and major changes in the public pension system are unlikely. It is also safe to forecast that the total per capita cost of providing for the health needs of the elderly will continue to rise relative to other prices, although what proportion of these costs the federal government will absorb is somewhat uncertain.

Defense, which accounts for 25 percent of gross total spending, is much more difficult to project in the face of the extraordinary developments in the Soviet bloc. Defense spending clearly depends on how those developments evolve. Nevertheless, procurement decisions made in the late 1980s will significantly affect the structure of our forces during the 1990s, and this too will influence future spending.

Interest at 14 percent of gross spending in 1989 will be determined by the future course of deficits and interest rates, both of which are extremely difficult to forecast over such a long period. But, with any luck at all, interest will grow slower than total spending or gross national product (GNP) over the rest of the 1990s.

The author is grateful to the Andrew W. Mellon Foundation for associated financial assistance.

TABLE 3-1

The Composition of Federal Spending, Fiscal Year 1989

(billions of dollars)

Category or Program	FY 1989 Outlays	Percentage of Gross Outlays	Percentage of GNP
National defense	303.5	25.1	5.9
Entitlements			
Pensions, disability, and health insurance			
Social security	230.4	19.1	4.5
Medicare	94.4	7.8	1.8
Federal civilian	31.8	2.6	0.6
Military	20.2	1.7	0.4
Other	5.1	0.4	0.1
Subtotal: pensions, disability, and health insurance	381.8	31.6	7.4
Other entitlements	161.8	13.4	3.1
Subtotal entitlements	543.6	45.0	10.5
Discretionary spending	191.0	15.8	3.7
Net interest	168.9	14.0	3.3
Gross spending	1,207.1	100.0	23.4
Offsetting receipts	−64.2	n.a.	−1.2
Total net spending	1,142.9	n.a.	22.2

NOTE: FY 1989, in billions: revenues = $990.8; deficit = $152.1; GNP = $5,152.8. n.a. = not applicable.
SOURCE: U.S. Congressional Budget Office, *The Economic and Budget Outlook: Fiscal Years 1991–1995* (Washington, D.C.: U.S. Government Printing Office, 1990).

Some of the most interesting policy issues will involve the 34 percent of spending not accounted for by defense, interest, social security, and Medicare. A multitude of programs reside in this "all other" category, and it is safe to predict that the time spent debating them will far exceed their relative quantitative importance. Significant policy changes in individual programs are, however, possible without having a dramatic impact on total spending.

The Recent Past

The past twenty years of fiscal history can be understood as the pursuit of four incompatible goals:

- maintaining a strong national defense
- fulfilling generous promises to a rapidly growing elderly population
- keeping taxes at the level of the early 1960s
- controlling the budget deficit

It is arithmetically impossible to achieve all four goals, and one or more have been violated at different times during the past two decades.

The root of the problem can be found in the late 1960s and early 1970s. Invented in 1965, Medicare has been a rapidly growing burden ever since. The real value of social security benefits was raised several times in the late 1960s and early 1970s, culminating with a very large increase in 1972 and the indexing of the program for inflation.

Initially, this very large increase in our promises to the elderly was financed without raising taxes. Payroll taxes were increased; but income taxes were reduced by a greater amount, and the total tax burden fell from a Vietnam peak of 20.1 percent of GNP in 1969 to 18.0 percent in 1972. During the period, 1962–1965, the average burden was 17.8 percent.

While the deficit reached 2 percent of GNP in 1972, the main change in budget policy over the period involved rapid cuts in defense spending from the Vietnam peak of 9.6 percent of GNP in 1968 to 6.9 percent in 1972. The defense cuts relative to GNP continued through 1978, when the ratio of defense spending to GNP reached 4.8 percent.

In other words, the very large increases in our long-term promises to the elderly were initially financed using a source of resources—the so-called Vietnam peace dividend—that could not be long lasting. Between 1968 and 1978, the rise in social security and Medicare's share of GNP rose by over 40 percent of the fall in defense's share. By the late 1970s, there was a broad consensus that our military forces were in deplorable shape, and spurred on by the Soviet invasion of Afghanistan and the Iranian hostage situation, President Carter launched a major defense buildup.

The Carter administration and the Congress attempted to finance the military buildup and the increasingly costly programs for the elderly by allowing inflation to raise the tax burden imposed by the tax system. Taxes rose from 17.7 percent of GNP in 1976 to 20.1 percent by 1980. Unfortunately for Carter, state and local taxes were rising at the same time, and the nation was rocked by a tax revolt that played an important role in the election of the antitax Ronald Reagan.

President Reagan proceeded as though there was no such thing as a budget constraint. He asked for massive tax cuts and the Congress responded by giving him somewhat more than he asked. If

65

the tax cuts of 1981 had been left in place, the tax burden would have fallen below that existing in the early 1960s, partly because the recession of 1982 so reduced inflation that a portion of the tax cut planned to offset inflation became a real tax cut instead. Simultaneously, the administration and the Congress accelerated the Carter defense buildup while cutting nondefense spending by only small amounts. Needless to say, the deficit soared.

The rest of the 1980s have been a struggle to correct the error of 1981. Taxes increased every year in the period 1982–1988, with particularly large increases in 1982, 1983, and 1984. Cumulatively, the increase amounted to more than 2 percent of GNP compared with where taxes were headed after the cuts of 1981. By 1989, revenues had reached 19.2 percent of GNP or about 7 percent higher than their average in 1962–1964.

Defense spending authority continued to rise rapidly through 1985 but, since that time, has been cut in real terms by almost 2 percent per year. Defense outlays, which lag somewhat behind spending authority, amounted to 5.3 percent of GNP in 1981, peaked at 6.5 percent in 1986, and fell to 5.9 percent by 1989.

The growth of nondefense, noninterest spending was constrained significantly after 1981 as the administration and the Congress attempted to lower the deficit. Social security was reformed in 1983 as it was about to go bankrupt. Benefits were cut marginally in the short run and more significantly in the long run, with an increase in the normal retirement age starting early in the next century. The Medicare payment system was reformed, and other entitlements were cut modestly. Nevertheless, entitlement spending's share of GNP ended the decade at 10.5 percent in 1989, only slightly less than the 10.7 percent of 1981. Rapidly rising health costs and a growing elderly population partly offset numerous cuts.

Nonentitlement programs were constrained more severely relative to GNP. Nondefense discretionary spending fell from 5.7 percent of GNP in 1981 to 3.7 percent in 1989, lower than that prevailing in the early 1960s. Grants to state and local governments were cut in absolute real terms, and their share of GNP fell by about one-third from its peak in 1978. This quantitative change was sufficient to cause a qualitative change in the nature of the relationship between the federal and the lower-level governments. State and local governments have become more independent and more important in public policy decision making.

Despite many examples of spending constraint in the 1980s, total net spending relative to GNP finished the decade only slightly below where it began. It was 22.2 percent in 1989 compared with 22.7

percent in 1981. A rapid rise in the interest bill from 2.3 to 3.3 of GNP because of huge deficits offset a large part of the relative decline in net noninterest spending from 20.4 to 18.9 percent of GNP between 1981 and 1989. The fall in noninterest civilian spending was even more remarkable—from 15.1 to 13.0 percent of GNP—given the inexorable rise in previous decades.

Of the four fiscal goals with which this chapter began, it is the fulfillment of our promises to the elderly that has remained relatively unscathed despite modest benefit reforms in 1983. In a sense we have come full circle, again cutting defense to help support the elderly just as we did in the late 1960s and early 1970s. Taxes, however, are above the level of the early 1960s, and the 1989 deficit at 3.0 percent of GNP is unusually high relative to deficits in the past during comparable periods of peace and prosperity.

The history of the 1980s clearly shows how hard it is to reduce deficits once they have arisen, even during a long economic recovery. Yet the Congress and the Reagan administration did a great deal to correct the error of 1981. Each time a deficit-reducing package was enacted, however, policy makers chose those deficit cuts that were least unpleasant politically. Each successive step has become harder, leading to the present total impasse over budget policy; the nation's budget process is in a total shambles. While enacting small amounts of real deficit reduction for 1990, the Congress and the new Bush administration have also resorted to a series of accounting tricks to make the measured deficit appear lower than it really is. Unfortunately, many of these gimmicks actually worsen the budget problems of the future. It is not a pleasant vantage point from which to view the spending issues of the 1990s. Nevertheless, as one must begin somewhere, a good starting point is provided by projections of the Congressional Budget Office (CBO) of the budget implications of a continuation of current policy.

The Budget Baseline for the 1990s

A budget baseline is a highly artificial construct. While it assumes a continuation of current budget policy, the term "current policy" must be defined, and this is somewhat controversial. The current CBO definition of current policy assumes no change in tax or entitlement laws. Where laws are temporary, they are generally allowed to expire, but there are a few minor exceptions where laws have been routinely extended. Nonentitlement or discretionary programs, including defense, are assumed to be held constant in real terms. Some believe that this creates an upward bias to spending, because the Congress

67

can claim a spending "cut" if it fails to provide a full inflation adjustment, even though nominal spending may rise.

This controversy is not, however, important to this analysis, which seeks only a starting point for the discussion. In this analysis, the term "policy changes" must be understood to imply legislated changes from this baseline. Although the baseline was computed before the deficit cuts enacted at the end of 1989, those cuts are relatively minor, and some are not long lasting.

The projections of spending and revenue are sensitive not only to legislated changes but also to assumptions about the future course of the economy and other crucially important factors. Obviously, unemployment rates are important determinants of spending on unemployment insurance and other income maintenance programs. Inflation determines the size of cost-of-living adjustments to pensions and other programs, and interest rates have an important effect on interest outlays.

Noneconomic factors are also significant. While economic assumptions may provide an estimate of the population eligible for a particular government program, it is also important to estimate how many eligibles will choose to participate. The weather will be important to the cost of agricultural subsidies, and the number of earthquakes and other natural disasters will affect spending on disaster assistance programs. One of the largest uncertainties facing us in the next decade is the eventual cost of the thrift bailout, which depends on both economic and other factors; and it is not hard to be wrong by over $50 billion.

Errors in forecasting economic and other variables may have as important an effect on spending and revenue as policy changes over the next decade. Moreover, the course of the economy will undoubtedly have a large impact on policy. If the economy grows more rapidly than expected, revenues will as well, and spending may then be higher or taxes lower than might be otherwise forecast.

The CBO budget projections assume that after a slowdown in 1990, the economy will grow at approximately 2.5 percent annually on average through 2000. Although this allows for an occasional recession, no attempt is made to forecast the timing of business fluctuations. The inflation rate is assumed to be almost constant at 4.3 percent from 1989 forward, and short- and long-run interest rates are assumed to decline slowly during the first half of the decade, reaching 6.1 and 7.6 percent respectively in 1994. They are then assumed to remain constant at those levels for the rest of the decade. The unemployment rate is assumed to stabilize at 5.6 percent.

The resulting revenue and spending projections are provided in tables 3–2 and 3–3. Small deviations from the underlying assumptions could cause large changes in the qualitative projections. For example, the projections imply that total spending will grow 5.6 percent annually between 1989 and 2000, while revenues grow 6.9 percent annually. The deficit falls from $152 billion in 1989 to $32 billion in 2000.[1] If outlays grow at one quarter of a percentage point per year faster than assumed while revenues grow at one quarter of a percentage point slower, the deficit in 2000 would be $139 billion or about the same as today's. If errors of the same magnitude go in the opposite direction, the deficit of $32 billion would be converted into a surplus of $76 billion. It is highly probable that errors of this size will occur.

Since we must begin somewhere, if we take the projections at face value they imply a gradual improvement in the deficit. This is the almost inevitable result of assuming that defense and all other discretionary programs are held constant in real terms, while the economy continues to grow because, under current law, tax revenues grow at about the same rate as the GNP.

Of the major spending categories, only entitlements grow faster than the economy, rising from 10.5 percent of GNP in 1989 to 11.3 percent in 2000. Were it not for the unusually slow growth of the elderly population in the 1990s, entitlements would grow even faster because of low birth rates during the Great Depression. If defense was, in fact, held constant in real terms, its share of GNP would fall from 5.9 percent in 1989 to 4.3 percent in 2000. The previous post–World War II low was 4.8 percent in 1978 and 1979.

A major reason for the improved deficit outlook in these projections coincides with the demographic trends that restrain entitlement growth. The social security system will experience rapidly growing annual surpluses for the entire period. By 2000, the annual social security surplus will reach $236 billion compared with $52 billion in 1989. All other operations of the government will experience a deficit that rises from $204 billion in 1989 to $268 billion in 2000, although it falls relative to GNP from 4.0 percent in 1989 to 2.5 percent by 2000.

Policy Issues

Although current policy projections suggest a gradually diminishing deficit, few would be happy with the implied path given that the underlying economic projections assume something close to full employment for the entire period. A few dissenters aside, the vast majority of analysts believe that the federal government should do more to contribute to national savings over the period.[2] The favorable demographic trends that allow deficit reduction for the rest of this

TABLE 3–2
BASELINE BUDGET PROJECTIONS, FISCAL YEARS 1989–2000
(billions of dollars)

	1989	1990	1991	1992	1993	1994	1995	1996	1997	1998	1999	2000
Outlays												
National defense	304	301	314	326	339	356	365	384	400	417	435	454
Nondefense discretionary spending	191	204	212	219	228	237	247	258	269	280	292	305
Entitlements and other mandatory spending	544	587	630	675	732	772	830	893	961	1,034	1,113	1,200
Net interest	169	180	189	195	203	209	216	222	228	233	238	240
Offsetting receipts	−64	−60	−63	−67	−71	−75	−81	−87	−93	−99	−105	−112
Total	1,142	1,212	1,282	1,348	1,430	1,500	1,576	1,670	1,766	1,867	1,974	2,088
Revenues	991	1,071	1,138	1,207	1,287	1,372	1,465	1,566	1,674	1,790	1,923	2,056
Deficit (−)	−152	−141	−144	−141	−143	−128	−111	−104	−92	−77	−51	−32
Social security a	52	65	75	86	99	113	127	144	163	185	209	236
Other	−204	−206	−219	−227	−242	−241	−238	−248	−255	−262	−260	−268

NOTE: 1989 data are actual data. The baseline was estimated before the results for fiscal 1989 were known and therefore assumes a slightly different base for the calculation. The effects of the 1990 deficit reduction package are not included.
a. Only those social security transactions that are off budget.
SOURCE: Congressional Budget Office.

TABLE 3–3
BASELINE BUDGET PROJECTIONS AS A PERCENTAGE OF GNP, FISCAL YEARS 1989–2000
(percent)

	1989	1990	1991	1992	1993	1994	1995	1996	1997	1998	1999	2000
Outlays												
National defense	5.9	5.5	5.4	5.2	5.1	5.0	4.8	4.7	4.6	4.5	4.4	4.3
Nondefense discretionary spending	3.7	3.7	3.6	3.5	3.4	3.3	3.3	3.2	3.1	3.0	3.0	2.9
Entitlements and other mandatory spending	10.5	10.7	10.8	10.8	11.0	10.9	10.9	11.0	11.1	11.2	11.2	11.3
Net interest	3.3	3.3	3.2	3.1	3.0	2.9	2.8	2.7	2.6	2.5	2.4	2.3
Offsetting receipts	−1.2	−1.1	−1.1	−1.1	−1.1	−1.1	−1.1	−1.1	−1.1	−1.1	−1.1	−1.1
Total	22.2	22.2	22.0	21.7	21.5	21.1	20.8	20.6	20.4	20.1	19.9	19.7
Revenues	19.2	19.6	19.5	19.4	19.3	19.3	19.3	19.3	19.3	19.3	19.4	19.4
Deficit (−)	−3.0	−2.6	−2.5	−2.3	−2.1	−1.8	−1.5	−1.3	−1.1	−0.8	−0.5	−0.3
Social security a	1.0	1.2	1.3	1.4	1.5	1.6	1.7	1.8	1.9	2.0	2.1	2.2
Other	−4.0	−3.8	−3.8	−3.6	−3.6	−3.4	−3.1	−3.1	−2.9	−2.8	−2.6	−2.5

NOTE: 1989 data are actual data. The baseline was estimated before the results for fiscal 1989 were known and therefore assumes a slightly different base for the calculation. The effects of the 1990 deficit reduction package are not included.
a. Only those social security transactions that are off budget.
SOURCE: Congressional Budget Office.

century under current policy are reversed early in the next century, as the ratio of the elderly to the working population begins to grow rapidly after 2005. There is general agreement that we should be doing more to help future workers cope with this burden and that the most direct approach to this problem is to move the budget into surplus.

The rest of this chapter asks whether much help can be expected from the spending side in achieving this end. Throughout the period there will be demands for spending increases in many programs, but there may be some savings as well. In what follows, important spending issues will be examined for each of the major functions of the budget.

Defense. The disintegration of the Soviet empire clearly represents the most important historical event since the 1940s, and, presuming that Gorbachev survives and that there is not a reversion to repression, the United States and its NATO allies are sure to cut defense spending substantially. The collapse of public support for maintaining high military spending may be so complete as to prevent policy makers from taking a rational approach to the pleasant task of reducing the defense burden, and it is very difficult to forecast how far the cuts will go. But, in a more rational world, the path to the future would be determined largely by where we have been in the past.

Defense spending has been on an incredible roller coaster during the 1980s. During the first half of the decade, the real value of budget authority grew about 8 percent per year. Since 1985, it has been declining at about 2 percent per year. Yet no change in foreign policy differentiated the first half of the 1980s from the second half, nor was there any significant change in defense strategy or even in tactics. The dramatic change in spending policy resulted solely from extreme budget stringency, not from a carefully prepared long-term plan.

Since 1985, budget authority for procurement has been cut disproportionately, actually declining in nominal terms from 32.8 percent of defense budget authority to 26.5 percent in 1989. Few weapons systems have been canceled, however. While the quantity to be purchased has been reduced in some cases, much of the saving comes from procuring new weapons more slowly. This often raises unit costs, because economies of scale in production cannot be fully exploited.

If tensions between East and West had remained at pre-Gorbachev levels and if long-term plans had not been changed significantly while the Congress continued to cut the defense budget, the nation would probably have ended up with an extremely unbalanced force structure by the mid-1990s. The forces might have had some modern weapons but insufficient funds to operate and maintain them satisfactorily. In late 1988, the CBO estimated that real spending increases of between 1 and 4 percent per year through 1994 were necessary to complete existing plans, with the actual growth depending on the speed with which remaining procurement plans were completed and the growth of operating costs.[3] There was no chance that the Congress would actually fund such spending growth, and, hence, the nation was headed for a highly inefficient composition of defense spending.

Fortunately, Gorbachev may have saved us from this fate. The collapse of communism in Eastern Europe has caused the Pentagon to rethink its strategy radically. The fact that defense spending increases would have been required to rationalize the plans of the 1980s, however, limits what can reasonably be quickly cut as the nation enters the 1990s.

As this is written, the planning process has just begun, and it is not known how it will evolve. It may, however, be possible to speculate crudely about the potential for major cuts in spending. Of course, our worldwide concerns extend far beyond the Soviet threat. We have major responsibilities in the Mideast, and we have to worry about Latin America and China. Although proper cost accounting is difficult, some have estimated that about 60 percent of our defense budget is devoted to the defense of Western Europe.

It obviously does not follow, however, that our defense budget can quickly be cut 60 percent. Gorbachev may fail, and a reactionary, repressive government may take over. Moreover, the costs of arbitrarily canceling procurement contracts and dismissing personnel are high, and it takes time to make major changes in the path of spending. Nevertheless, because risks have been reduced substantially, major reductions in forces and in weapons procurement should be possible, perhaps countered by some strengthening of our reserve forces to guard against increased future risks.

Developing a rational plan will be a considerable intellectual challenge. We have a wide variety of options for structuring our forces during a post–cold war period. But it may be even more of a challenge to get the Congress, which will be subjected to conflicting pressures, to accept a rational plan. If improvements continue in Eastern Europe, the public will demand some very large cuts but at the same time will be reluctant to lose defense-related jobs in their districts. This conflict probably means that, in the end, we shall not cut efficiently, but we are almost certain to cut substantially.

Given the immense uncertainties about future developments in the Soviet Union and Eastern Europe and about how U.S. defense budgeting reacts to those developments, speculation about the precise course of defense spending in the 1990s may be foolish, but at the risk of error, a few plausible scenarios might be useful.

The Pentagon's planning will identify specific cuts in procurement, research, and personnel. Military planners will then be pushed to cut further by the Office of Management and Budget, and whatever the president decides to recommend will probably be cut yet again by the Congress. To obtain an upper bound for the projections, however, we might find it useful to begin with the Pentagon's likely wish list. At the time of writing, newspaper accounts of Secretary Cheney's directions to the military are somewhat imprecise, but they seem to imply an average real decline of about 2 percent per year in defense budget authority between 1990 and 1994.

If a 3 percent rate of decline is used under the reasonable assumption that the Pentagon will not get everything that it wants, defense outlays would slightly exceed $315 billion in 1994 and would absorb 4.4 percent of GNP compared with 5.0 percent in the baseline case. If all else remained equal—an unlikely event—the total budget deficit in 1994 would fall from 1.8 to 1.2 percent of GNP.

While I think it reasonable to use this as an upper bound for defense spending if reforms continue in the Soviet bloc, the assumed cuts are very large and will have a significant impact on the fortunes of defense-related companies and specific geographical areas. The cuts also imply a significant reduction in military personnel. Nevertheless, the cuts do appear to be politically feasible in an era when defense spending will have lost public support. Between the peak of Vietnam spending in 1968 and 1972, defense's share of GNP fell by a much greater 2.7 percentage points and continued to fall by another 2.1 percentage points by 1978. The cut implied here is only about 1 percent of GNP compared with 1990 levels and 2.1 percentage points from the recent peak of 6.5 percent in 1986.

If, after 1994, defense spending holds constant in real terms, its share of GNP will fall to 3.8 percent in 2000 compared with a baseline level of 4.3 percent. All else equal, the baseline deficit projected to equal 0.3 percent of GNP would be converted to a surplus of 0.2 percent of GNP, although the non–social security deficit would still equal 1.7 percent of GNP.

Some experts believe that events in Eastern Europe will allow a much greater cut in defense spending than the upper-bound projection implies. William Kaufman, for example, has suggested a path for spending that would lower defense outlays to about the same level as assumed above for 1994 but then continue to reduce defense's share of GNP until it reached about 1.6 percent in 1999 in his most Draconian scenario. This level is less than one-half of what was assumed in the upper-bound projection.

While such a cut would allow a substantial unified surplus in 2000, all else equal, and would more than eliminate the deficit on non–social security operations, it is probably a larger cut than future administrations and Congresses would accept. It assumes that the world remains very peaceful indeed through the end of the decade—an unrealistic suspension of Murphy's Law.

Another possible scenario would have the Congress simply freeze nominal spending authority. That would impose a 4.3 percent annual decline, given the baseline's inflation assumption, or a somewhat greater decline than proposed by Kaufman initially but a lesser decline over the entire decade. Defense outlays would fall to 4.0 percent of GNP by 1994 and to 2.6 percent by the year 2000. All else equal, the projected unified surplus in 2000 would be 1.4 percent of GNP, or about two-thirds of the surplus in social security.

It is, of course, somewhat mindless to discuss defense policy purely in terms of different rates of real decline in spending. It should be discussed in the context of the evolution of our foreign policy and the risks implied by that policy. Once an acceptable level of risk is defined, it should then be translated into a specific force structure that could be costed out. Given the immense complexity and uncertainties inherent in such an analysis, it is impossible to pursue here. Unfortunately, such an analysis is also probably too complex for the Congress to apply rationally, which will probably resort to rules of thumb based on arbitrary real declines in spending. Because of the extraordinary information needs for a more sophisticated analysis, resorting to rules of thumb is not irrational. If our forces seem to be evolving inappropriately under arbitrary rules of thumb and risks begin to grow or drop rapidly, midcourse corrections can then be implemented.

Entitlements and Other Mandatory Spending. In 1989, social security, Medicare, and Medicaid accounted for about two-thirds of total spending in this category, and in the baseline projections their share is projected to grow to over 70 percent by 1994, despite the favorable demographics. The rapidly increasing cost of providing health care is the main reason for this growth, and social security's share of the total will actually decline slightly over the period. Nevertheless, social security will remain the largest civilian program throughout the 1990s.

Social Security. Without a doubt, social security is the most popular government program ever invented, making it difficult to debate cutting it. Reductions in the 1990s are made even more unlikely, however, by projected large annual surpluses for the social security trust funds throughout the decade resulting from the unusually slow growth of the elderly population and the payroll tax increases of the late 1970s and early 1980s.

The elderly population will again begin to grow rapidly after 2005, however, while the labor force will be growing very slowly because of the fall in birth rates after the late 1950s. In an ideal world, the 1990s would be used to prepare for this future increase in the social security burden, but our political system is not noted for its farsightedness, and major changes in the system are unlikely.

Social security outlays start at about 4.5 percent of GNP in 1989 and then grow only slightly less rapidly than the economy, reaching a low of 4.4 percent of GNP in 2005. After that they grow rapidly to a peak of about 6.8 percent of GNP in 2035. It is projected that under current law, the system will be bankrupt shortly before the middle of the century. These estimates are based on the II-B assumptions of the trustees of the social security system, which differ slightly from the assumptions underlying the baseline projections in the earlier discussion.[4]

Note that the rise in social security of slightly more than 2 percent of GNP is not enormous, actually falling short of possible defense savings during the 1990s. Nevertheless, the increased burden is significant enough that it is worth debating whether society wants to devote a growing share of GNP to the elderly's pensions, with so many other claims on the nation's resources.

The elderly, who were among the country's neediest groups as recently as the early 1960s, have been doing very well recently, largely because of increases in social security in the late 1960s and early 1970s. Their poverty rate in 1987 at 12.2 percent is now lower than the average of 13.5 percent for the entire population, and their after-tax income per household member is higher. Their mean total household income is lower, however, because their average household size is smaller.

Debate over how generous public pensions should be is impossible without simultaneous consideration of public policy toward pensions other than social security. Over 42 percent of civilian workers were covered by employer- or union-provided pension plans in the late 1980s, and their assets have been growing rapidly. A few years ago, it appeared that coverage would continue to grow, but public policy has recently become less favorable, especially toward defined benefit plans. Antidiscrimination rules and ERISA regulations, intended to foster equitable and reliable private pension plans, may be having the perverse effect of discouraging employers, and many plans are being terminated. Defined contribution plans are in less trouble, but even here the 1986 tax reform reduced the appeal of IRAs.

Clearly, recent trends should be reviewed and debated in the early 1990s. While discouraging defined benefit plans may well be desirable, we should develop a more comprehensive approach to encouraging, or at least not discouraging, defined contribution plans.

If private pensions continue to grow, it will be somewhat easier to argue for reduced replacement rates under social security, especially for the more affluent. There are a number of appealing options for achieving this goal.

Currently, only one-half of social security benefits above an income threshold of $25,000 for single returns and $32,000 for joint returns are put in the tax base. If social security were taxed like private pensions, over 85 percent of the benefit would be put in the tax base currently. The 15 percent exemption reflects a credit for the benefit financed by employee contributions out of after-tax income. Using the 85 percent figure and eliminating the threshold would raise tax revenues by over $25 billion in 1994. If the current thresholds were retained, the revenue gain falls to $5.3 billion. In both cases, the after-tax replacement rate would be reduced significantly only for the more affluent. Even if the income threshold is removed, elderly below the poverty line would not be affected at all, and those somewhat above the line would be affected very little. The recent experience with taxing the affluent elderly for catastrophic health benefits, however, suggests that this reasonable option would face tough sledding politically.

A different method for reducing replacement rates is to increase the age at which full benefits are received somewhat faster and to a greater extent than scheduled in current law. Currently, that normal retirement age will be increased to sixty-six slowly during the first decade of the next century. There is then a ten-year hiatus, after which it will again be increased slowly to age sixty-seven in 2027. Beneficiaries will still be allowed to retire as early as age sixty-two, but depending on the age chosen, there will be an actuarially appropriate reduction in benefits. Thus, an increase in the normal retirement age is equivalent to altering the benefit formula, so that the replacement rate is reduced at any specific age of retirement.

If, instead of the current approach, the normal retirement age were raised slowly and steadily after 2003 so that it reached age seventy in 2037, the savings in social security benefits would amount to roughly 1 percent of GNP by the middle of the next century. An appealing attribute of this option is that it would reduce the social security burden at about the same time that it is peaking relative to GNP.

Although such an option would not save anything during the 1990s, it should be debated during that decade to give those near retirement plenty of time to adjust their plans. Provoking such a debate while the system is in surplus, however, will be very difficult. It is remarkable that the normal retirement age was increased in the 1983 reforms, since the increase was not required to cure the short-run financing problem and had not been recommended by the Greenspan Commission, appointed to recommend solutions for the short-run problem.

An increase in the normal retirement age would reduce the replacement rate at any specific age of retirement for rich and poor alike. The effect on the poor may be an important factor limiting its appeal, and the same problem often afflicts other proposals for reducing the social security burden, such as modifications of cost of living adjustments. If poor retirees were treated more generously by enhancing Supplemental Security Income (SSI) benefits, the social security system might be easier to reform. Currently, many of the elderly poor are prevented from participating in SSI by an unrealistically stringent asset test ($2,000 for a single person and $3,000 for a couple). That requirement should be made more lenient in the 1990s, and this step should be taken even before considering increases in SSI benefits. A relaxation of the asset test is very expensive, however, and that will inhibit its adoption.

Unfortunately, most social security debates of the 1990s will likely involve options for increasing rather than decreasing benefits. Congress now faces strong pressure to remove the annual social security surplus from the deficit concept targeted in the budget process. The proposal is well intended. It is hoped that if the seriousness of the deficit in the non–social security operations of the government were no longer obscured by partially offsetting it with the large social security surplus, then we would make more vigorous attempts to reduce it.

Unfortunately, if social security is removed from the targeted deficit, social security benefit increases or payroll tax reductions will no longer count against the official deficit, perhaps creating a dangerous loss of budget discipline in the social security system. The problem might be countered by establishing rigid rules for ensuring the financing of benefit increases in the short and long run, as

Chairman Dan Rostenkowski has recently proposed. But any rule can be changed by a majority of the Congress, and therefore, restraining rules are not very reliable.

Among the benefit liberalizations that might be debated are the elimination of the requirement that workers under age seventy retire before receiving full benefits, a cure for the illegitimate claims of the notch babies,[5] and a reduction in the inequitable treatment of working wives compared with traditional housewives. There could even be a movement to eliminate the increase in the retirement age contained in the 1983 reforms. In the two other historical instances in which surpluses developed in the trust funds—during World War II and in the 1960s—benefits were liberalized soon after.

Unfortunately, the social security program cannot be debated like any other program of government. Granted, we have a moral contract not to change the benefit structure abruptly, but moral contracts should be subject to renegotiation just as legal contracts are when conditions change. And conditions have changed dramatically and will change further in the twenty-first century. On average, the elderly are much more affluent than they once were, and continuing the high level of generosity will impose a significant burden on the virtually stagnant labor force of the future. No problem occurs in maintaining the current absolute value of real benefits presuming that the economy continues to grow. The question is how fast real benefits should be increased. For a single worker, earning the average wage over his or her lifetime, the before-tax replacement rate is now about 42 percent at age sixty-five (63 percent with a dependent spouse). Even though the absolute real value of benefits will rise, the rate will gradually fall to about 36 percent in 2030 because of the increase in the normal retirement age. It can be raised, however, if the worker chooses to work longer.[6] This leaves it slightly above the levels of the 1950s and 1960s when the elderly were much less affluent. The key question is whether the nation can continue to afford this generosity with so many competing claims on our resources.

Health Issues. The two major health programs of the federal government, Medicare and Medicaid, have been growing at a tremendous rate, both because of increases in the eligible population and because of soaring health costs. Soon after the turn of the century, Medicare is expected to be larger than the social security program.

In 1975, when Medicare and Medicaid were about ten years old, they absorbed about 1.3 percent of GNP compared with social security's 4.1 percent. By 1985, ten years later, they absorbed 2.4 percent

79

compared with social security's 4.7 percent. The same sort of explosive cost growth is afflicting private insurance plans, and in the late 1980s, the increased costs of employer plans constituted a large portion of total compensation growth. Still, many Americans are left with no insurance at all. It is clear that this extraordinary growth in the nation's health costs cannot be allowed to continue indefinitely, but whether the problem becomes severe enough to provoke a radical reform in the 1990s is open to question. We have only three broad categories of options for slowing the growth of the public component of health costs. Either the array of benefits provided must be cut, providers must be paid less, or recipients must pay a larger share of the costs.

In the 1980s, reforms focused on reducing payments to providers. The Medicare reimbursement system for hospitals was reformed significantly in the mid-1980s as payments were based on the problem being treated rather than on the cost of treatment. Although the new system seems to have saved considerable amounts, it is too soon to evaluate it definitively. Moreover, while attempts were made to limit fees paid to physicians, these efforts were clearly unsuccessful, as payments continued to grow rapidly. Physicians were perhaps gaming the system by prescribing more treatments and tests, but, it was also argued, the growing threat of malpractice suits played an important role in increasing costs.

In 1989 a comprehensive fee schedule for physicians was enacted in a very important reform of the system. We shall, however, be well into the 1990s before knowing whether the new system is working effectively.

It is, of course, difficult to limit the fees paid to providers without simultaneously increasing the amounts paid by recipients. The new hospital reimbursement system, for example, reduces the length of stay, but hospitals respond by increasing the per day charge, thus increasing Medicare's deductible.

The 1990s are sure to see an intense debate over where the system should go next. Although efforts to limit the growth of provider payments and to increase recipient payments through greater premiums for physician insurance (Part B of Medicare) will continue, most of the debate will be focused on increasing rather than on decreasing benefits as the relative price of medical services continues to rise.

Efforts will continue to cover those now uncovered by health insurance, but this is more likely to be accomplished by mandating that employers provide coverage rather than through additional on-budget expenditures. The problem of providing coverage for medical catastrophes is certain to be revisited, but the most important, and potentially most costly, issue will be coverage for long-term medical care.

In recent years, more and more long-term care has been provided through the Medicaid program after recipients have become sufficiently impoverished to qualify, sometimes by divesting assets. As a result, Medicaid has become more and more a program for the elderly. Attempts, some already enacted, to reduce the degree of impoverishment necessary by spouses will continue and may extend to the recipients themselves.

As tensions between rising costs and demand for new benefits intensify, national health insurance will be debated more seriously. The nature of the debate is sure to change as the possibility of using national health insurance to guarantee equal access to health care falls in importance relative to the potential for using such a system to ration care and to control the incomes of providers. Recent interest in such a system has risen, as it appears that countries with national programs, such as Canada and the United Kingdom, spend less of their GNP on health care than we do. In addition, support for national health insurance has been growing among major corporations that see their provision of health insurance putting them at a competitive disadvantage against foreign competition and against smaller, less generous domestic firms.

The debate over such a radical reform will probably take more than a decade to resolve. It is safe to forecast, however, that the debate will rage on and that the share of GNP spent publicly and privately on health care will be higher at the end of the decade than it is currently. A very large part, if not all, of the peace dividend, if it materializes, will probably be spent in this area.

Other Entitlements. Non-means tested entitlements discussed above have provided an important source of income for the poverty population. Contrary to the perceptions of the public, though, welfare or means-tested programs explicitly directed at the poor have never constituted an important part of federal spending. Through the 1980s, they composed about 8 percent of total spending and roughly one-third of that amount was devoted to Medicaid.

During the 1980s non-Medicaid welfare absorbed a peak of 1.3 percent of GNP in 1981, declining to a little more than 1 percent of GNP by the end of the decade. The decline resulted from the long economic recovery and some cutbacks in the programs.

These programs, especially those focused on children, are likely to be debated intensely in the 1990s. About 20 percent of our children live in poverty and Aid to Families with Dependent Children, one of the few entitlements not indexed for inflation, has been allowed to erode in real terms since the 1970s. Debate will continue on things such as work requirements and child support enforcement, but increases in the generosity of payments are likely to be debated as well. Welfare, not including Medicaid, however, starts out being such a small part of the budget that significant increases are possible without having an important effect on the trend of total spending in the 1990s.

Farm price supports soared in the mid-1980s, but new farm legislation combined with the lingering effects of the 1988 drought reduced payments to 0.2 percent of GNP in 1989. While international negotiations in the 1990s may reduce the competitive subsidization of farmers in the developed world, it will not be easy, and such subsidies may soar yet again.

Outside social security and Medicare, the largest entitlement spending of the 1990s will be the continued bailout of the thrift industry. The $50 billion of borrowing authority created for this purpose will clearly not be sufficient, and the net, public cost of the program could easily double before the end of the decade. Most of the cost will accrue off budget, but interest costs will be recorded on budget. These will be substantial, and their increase could exceed any increase in the generosity of welfare benefits. For the most part, the economic costs were imposed in the past when bad loans were made, but some costs will continue because of subsidies paid to those taking over sick thrifts. Huge sales of seized assets are also likely to affect capital markets and markets for real estate because of market imperfections. Therefore the bailout will have some real effects for many years to come. Simply managing this vast effort will occupy a large portion of our decision-making resources over the next decade and will detract from sensible decision making in other areas.

Will any new entitlements be created outside the health area in the next decade? Budget pressures will probably slow any dramatic new initiatives. The one candidate for entitlement status is child care, but this is more likely to be handled by nonentitlement spending except for some improvement in the earned-income credit. While grants to state and local governments for this purpose will be enhanced, access to benefits will probably depend on location rather than on rules defining eligibility.

Interest on the National Debt. Interest on the national debt now constitutes about 14 percent of gross total spending or about 3.3 percent of GNP. If the budget deficit remains on a declining path relative to GNP and if interest rates do not soar, interest should begin to diminish both as a share of total spending and as a share of GNP during the 1990s. The cost of the thrift bailout, however, will retard its decline.

Interest and debt management are seldom debated publicly. The size of the national debt and the associated interest cost are regarded simply as the indirect result of all our other budget decisions. Because a change in debt management practices could perhaps reduce interest costs by $1–2 billion—particularly given the extreme difficulty of extracting that amount of money from other programs—debt management should clearly be debated with more energy.

The Treasury, for example, without debate raised the average maturity of the public debt from a low of two years and seven months in 1976 to five years and nine months in 1988. With the exception of brief periods in the late 1970s and early 1980s, short-term interest rates were lower than long-term rates for the entire period, and the lengthening of the debt imposed significant extra interest costs. Although some lengthening was called for, the undebated question was, How much and when? given that the administration was rightly predicting that long rates would fall for much of this period.

Much more radical approaches to debt management could be considered. Zero-coupon bonds could be issued in significant quantities rather than letting others profit from separately selling the rights to the coupons and principal from existing Treasuries. More radically, price-indexed bonds, foreign currency bonds, and even gold bonds could be considered. All create significant risks for the Treasury, but a diversity of issues should lower interest costs significantly in the very long run. Perhaps the increased risk is not worth the saving, but the issue deserves more attention in the 1990s as interest costs approach and will probably exceed $200 billion before the decade is over.

Ironically, the debate will probably be inhibited by our budget process. Gramm-Rudman-Hollings has greatly shortened the time horizon of the Congress, and long-term savings are not of much interest. Moreover, the risks make it hard for OMB and CBO to give Ways and Means and Senate Finance any credit for savings associated with changes in debt management policies, even for the five-year period over which most budget projections are made. Understandably, the Congress is unwilling to consider controversial changes for which no credit is given and which could turn out to be very costly in the short run. The French government learned about such risks when it had to redeem gold bonds just as the price of gold neared its peak a decade ago.

Other Spending Issues. Both the Reagan and the Bush administrations have recommended terminating a number of programs such as the Economic Development Administration, urban mass transit grants, and the Appalachian Regional Commission. Certainly such program terminations should continue to be debated in the 1990s, but since they have largely survived the assaults of two presidents, it is hard to be optimistic that significant savings can be obtained from this source, as worthy as many of the cuts may be.

Meanwhile, demands are growing for increased spending in the nondefense discretionary part of the budget, partly because it bore much of the brunt of spending stringency in the 1980s. As already noted, its share of GNP fell from 5.9 percent in 1980 to 3.7 percent in 1989, and its share of gross total spending fell from 23.7 percent to 15.8 percent over the same period. Much of the reduction involved grants to state and local governments, which had reached a high of 3½ percent of GNP in 1978 but which had fallen to about 2¼ percent of GNP by 1989. This decline, which constituted one of the most important reforms in civilian spending in the 1980s, may now be about to be reversed, as the Congress is considering new, highly categorical grants in numerous fields such as education, infrastructure, and child care. Categorical grants may also be contemplated for the growing troubles of the underclass, for other difficulties afflicting our inner cities, and, of course, for drug problems and crime prevention.

Many new spending proposals, in fact, involve functions traditionally undertaken largely at the state and local level. Of these, both the Bush administration and the Congress agree that high priority should be given to educational expenditures. In fiscal 1989, federal spending on primary, secondary, and vocational spending amounted to a little over $9 billion, or less than 1 percent of total spending. About $10 billion was spent on higher education. Even if such spending were increased at a real rate of 5 percent per year through the 1990s—a rate far higher than is likely to be proposed by the administration or than seems probable—less than 0.2 percent more of GNP would be absorbed by this function. While the issue will be hotly debated in the 1990s, the result is unlikely to be of significant importance to federal spending trends relative to many of the entitlement issues. Put another way, minor reforms in entitlements could theoretically release sufficient resources for major increases in the education budget.

Another issue receiving increased attention is the nation's infrastructure of public investments. To the extent that the debate centers on highways, bridges, and sewer systems, the issue concerns projects largely funded by state and local governments, supplemented by federal grants.

Between 1980 and 1987, the federal government's spending on infrastructure remained stagnant, while state and local spending doubled. Spending by all levels of government increased about 25 percent in real terms. Stagnation in the federal government's contribution was not all bad, because spending on physical investments has traditionally constituted a large share of the government's pork barrel, with enormous waste, especially on water projects. Therefore, politicians' claims that infrastructure needs are enormous should be viewed with considerable skepticism.

Yet some areas of investment may yield high returns, although the size of such investments appears to be quite small. It is estimated, for example, that an extra $2 billion spent annually on maintaining federally aided highways would yield returns of between 30 and 40 percent. In contrast, the extra $9 billion per year to enhance highway capacity, demanded by some, might yield only 1 percent annually nationwide, although particular projects may be more productive.

Clearly, infrastructure investment should be approached cautiously and requires careful cost-benefit analysis. A useful test is to ask whether user fees could be levied to finance projects. Although some have argued, for example, that large amounts should be spent to repair aging locks and dams on waterways, the Department of Transportion has estimated that if user fees were levied to pay only operating and maintenance costs, four of twelve waterway segments would no longer be commercially viable.[7]

The conclusions are quite obvious to this analyst. Yes, there is an infrastructure problem, but it is often greatly exaggerated. State and local government has been rising to the challenge, and it is preferable to leave the bulk of the financial responsibility there. They are better able to judge costs and benefits for most projects. The federal government may have to take on some extra responsibility in the maintenance of some highway and other projects whose construction it encouraged initially, and in a few areas the projects of lower-level governments have beneficial spillovers into other states. Because public works are so popular with politicians, however, the real danger is that we shall spend too much rather than too little.

In the CBO baseline, which assumes constant real spending in the nondefense discretionary component of the budget, its share of GNP falls from 3.7 percent of GNP in 1989 to 2.9 percent in 2000, thereby contributing about 30 percent of the decline in the baseline deficit from 3.0 to 0.3 percent of GNP. The demands just discussed are likely to lead to real spending increases in this area, however.

85

Whether the increases will be sufficient to maintain this function's share of GNP is more questionable. My guess is that they will not be and that this function will contribute to lowering total spending relative to GNP. The reduction in its share, however, will not be nearly as great in the 1990s as implied by the baseline.

Off-Budget Spending Issues. Clearly the federal budget will remain stringent during the 1990s, even if a sizable peace dividend materializes. The demands for increased government activism are intensifying, and there will be a strong temptation to spend the peace dividend many times. Under these conditions many initiatives will be undertaken to move governmental activism off budget.

One can expect increased regulation mandating that businesses and state and local governments provide certain benefits, especially in improving the environment, and the number of government-sponsored enterprises is likely to grow. A very large new one may soon be created to resolve the cash flow problem facing the thrift bailout. More loan guarantee programs are likely to be created, along with a temptation to solve our agricultural problems through crop limitations rather than through on-budget subsidies.

These are pernicious trends because off-budget initiatives are inherently more difficult to control than on-budget activities, which are difficult enough. In the extreme, the government may create a large number of contingent liabilities and thus risk another fiasco comparable to the thrift bailout.

Conclusions

Much of the above discussion is based on a weak foundation. The analysis has proceeded as though the assumptions underlying baseline projections will be more or less accurate. Conceivably, errors in the baseline assumptions will have a more important effect on future budgets than any of the policy issues discussed here. But those errors could go in either a favorable or an unfavorable direction.

If the baseline turns out to be fairly accurate and if a sizable peace dividend materializes, however, the slow growth of the elderly population should make the budget pressures of the 1990s much less than those of the 1980s. Indeed, if the deficit cannot be substantially reduced in the 1990s, it is unlikely ever to be reduced, as demographic pressures mount in the twenty-first century.

The analysis of this paper suggests further that the nation could move to a significant unified budget surplus by the turn of the century without significant tax increases if nondefense spending could be kept to baseline levels. This is unlikely, however, and the peace dividend may yet fail to materialize. We have seen the intense demands for spending above baseline levels in a number of areas, and the number of politically feasible cuts is minimal.

The most serious entitlement demands are for increased health care. The desire to cover the uninsured and to provide extra benefits for catastrophic and long-term care will be difficult to ignore. Strong arguments will also be made to increase the generosity of child welfare programs, and the ultimate cost of the thrift bailout is likely to soar beyond current estimates. In addition, spending for social security could increase, even though long-term reductions could legitimately be debated. A consensus also seems to be growing that greater spending is desirable in various nondefense discretionary programs, especially in education and the infrastructure, although these are likely to be minor relative to entitlement growth.

Not only pessimists might conclude that we will have to have tax increases or significant deficits throughout the decade. The worst of all worlds will result if the error of the late 1960s and early 1970s is repeated, and the peace dividend, which is sure to end eventually, is used to finance a permanent increase in entitlements for the elderly, whose costs are sure to soar in the twenty-first century.

Yet none of these pessimistic observations should obscure the basic point that total spending pressures in the 1990s should be less than those of previous decades. If we were starting with a more prudent budget base, the 1990s would be quite pleasant. Given that we start with a large deficit, the nation has a golden opportunity to correct the errors of the 1980s. It is, in fact, hard to believe that the deficit will grow relative to GNP in the 1990s unless the peace dividend disappears completely. This is a small consolation, because the deficit will probably not decline as fast as most of us would like. But budget analysts are accustomed to small consolations.

4
Alternative Views of the Future

Commentary by Bill Gradison, G. William Hoagland,
Lawrence J. Korb, John H. Makin, and Norman J. Ornstein

BILL GRADISON: Focusing on the long term would give an entirely incorrect picture of the way decisions are made on fiscal issues. Therefore, it might be useful to talk about what may happen, or at least what is likely to be discussed where I work.

We will continue to see highly imaginative uses of budgetary gimmicks. It is quite extraordinary now, as I go into my eighth year on the Budget Committee, to see the development of this art form, and the fact that it is used so effectively by so many different players of both parties, both houses, and by both the executive and the legislative branches.

Two that particularly intrigue me now because of the magnitudes of their possible impact, involve major timing shifts. One of the ways in which the Medicare target for savings, for example, was met in the current fiscal year was to shift some of the payment for hospitals and other providers from fiscal 1990 into fiscal 1991. The providers were quite happy with this because late payment did not permanently reduce the base on which increases would be calculated. It seems quite likely that one of the ways the targets will be met in part in 1991 is to pay these folks when they originally expected to be paid, which is in 1990 for 1990 bills; this reduces the deficit in 1991.

Lee Hamilton quite properly has reminded us that Gramm-Rudman has nothing to do with reducing the deficit but only reducing the projected deficit. I would keep a particular eye on the discussion about financing the savings and loan, the so-called working capital fund.

Having favored budget financing and basically lost, I have a bit of a prejudice here. But the opportunity for fun and games is quite extraordinary. Just before the end of the fiscal year, these agencies could go through the Federal Financing Bank, raise far more than they needed from working capital—after all, anything you borrow in this current year does not make any difference for Gramm-Rudman purposes—and then pay enough of it back in the following year, that is, the excess that you really did not need to resolve cases, to give the appearance of meeting the targets.

But then perhaps you will say this means we have to focus on budget reform. I am a skeptic about budget reform. Most of it is hype and idle tinkering, and I do not take it seriously. But some ideas are downright dangerous, such as taking social security off budget, off the Gramm-Rudman calculations, which would clearly lead to higher spending, a greater federal borrowing, and less control over the budget than we have now—if that is possible.

Larry Korb no doubt will talk more about this, but it is reasonable to expect much discussion about what to do with the peace dividend. I consider the peace dividend nonexistent, or if it existed, we have had it for five years and have not noticed much pleasure from it. This is the fifth consecutive year in which real defense spending declined. Not until the last few months did I hear renewed use of the term "peace dividend," something which I thought went out of style following the Vietnam War.

One of the great lessons today is that the budget is no longer even being discussed seriously as a tool for macroeconomic policy. Maybe it should, maybe it should not. I am skeptical about how successful we were when we did try to use it and about the timing of the effects of what we actually did.

But as a practical matter our budgetary focus increases the burden of the Federal Reserve. I would feel much happier about the criticisms of the Federal Reserve and the argument that we should make greater use of fiscal policy if I thought fiscal policy had a decent track record. While monetary policy is not perfection, it is in a totally different league in its degree of effectiveness.

I am intrigued with the need for changes in the tax system. I am worried about whether the Tax Reform Act of 1986 will be sustained. Having been a supporter of it and lived through it, I think that it was a fluke that all those changes were made.

In other words, what started as reform became a revolution, and reactions to revolution have some precedent in history, maybe even in the tax field. The great irony is that the shaky consensus that held together the Tax Reform Act of 1986, base broadening and rate reduction, may well be tested on the issues of capital gains and individual retirement accounts (IRAs) or some kind of a tax free savings account, not exactly where one might have expected the testing of that general trade-off.

The bottom line is that as long as the government viewed broadly, the executive and congressional branches together, does not have to pay a price for its failure to deal effectively with deficit and fiscal issues, not much will happen. I see absolutely no evidence from the past or from the current debate or from election results that there is a political price to pay for the present state of affairs, none whatsoever.

Regarding the economic price we seem able to find people willing to lend us the money we need. They do not pay much attention to these little inside games about bookkeeping and record keeping. They are interested in what our net borrowing will be in the course of the year, but the game playing, although it involves large amounts of money, like the savings and loan situation, has not had as serious an impact as external shocks through the credit markets. Such signals might force events in the political system; that is, the decisions will probably be made on somewhat of a business-as-usual basis with one eye on the economy but maybe more of an eye on the upcoming elections.

One final note regarding Senator Moynihan's interesting proposals. At bottom, his ideas are responsive to two legitimate concerns, both to do with politics in the best sense of the word. First, between now and about the year 2010 or 2015, even if social security is properly funded and not all invested in the current government expenditures, would it be possible for Congress to avoid the temptation to use that for benefit increases of one kind or other in the budget—the federal general benefit structure, the elimination of the earnings test, or the so-called notch, all the hot buttons? That is a legitimate point to raise and discuss. It is a question of degree, how large a reserve can be built and sustained without being used for short-term purposes.

Second, a much more difficult question, what should the structure of the tax system be? The big tax increases recently have been in payroll taxes, and the public has tolerated this remarkably well over a long period. My sense, particularly from contact with small business constituents, is that we may be nearing the end of the road on that. And it is not entirely clear that the increases in the payroll tax that just took effect and those scheduled to take effect under current law will be possible.

The notion of a freeze or rollback of payroll taxes is a relatively popular idea. But just to stop at that point is irresponsible because it simply would lead to a larger deficit. To suggest taking away any major source of revenue, whether it is income tax or payroll tax or whatever, without suggesting how that be filled, either through spending cuts or substitution of another tax, is the point yet to be raised.

I look forward to hearing more from Senator Moynihan about

the second stage. He has the first stage of his rocket well up in the air. But to carry that analogy one step further, the people will go ballistic if they find that this tax cut that sounds so great is to be accompanied by a tax increase somewhere else.

G. WILLIAM HOAGLAND: As a staff person I have to make the usual advertisement about how my views are my own and in no way should be inferred to represent those of any member of the Senate Budget Committee, particularly its ranking minority member, Senator Domenici.

I want to review briefly three things: the 1980s from a staff person's perspective, the near term regarding the budget, and the general outlook for the 1990s.

In the end the economic historians will assess the successes or failures of the 1980s, not in 1990 but down the road. But if you were to look at and listen to the various commentaries—not to John Makin's editorials—you would see this decade has been full of deceitfulness, greed, selfishness, consumption, and irresponsible public officials.

As one who played a minimal role in this decade of deceit, with at least a good ringside seat, I feel compelled to defend the 1980s a bit. No single issue clearly dominated the discussion of the decade as much as the federal budget deficit. And I do not mean to minimize the importance of the federal deficit during this period, but economic historians will look back and write that this was a decade of immense transition and advances. The paradox of this decade is that those factors that brought about some of these advances are precisely those same factors that seem to be most disruptive.

The decade, as many of you will recall from a *Time* cover of the year 1980, began enmeshed in apocalyptic thinking of whether capitalism is working. But the decade ended with the second longest economic expansion and clearly the unabashed triumph of Western economic and political liberalism throughout the world.

Clearly and arguably one of the costs of this transition has been the accumulation of debt, and we should not minimize that. But the decade ended about where it began. Our spending was 22.2 percent of GNP in 1980, and most recent CBO estimates show an identical figure for 1990. Revenues in fact were 19.4 percent of GNP in 1980 and ended at 19.6 percent of GNP in 1989.

Clearly we were at a 2.8 percent deficit in 1980, 2.5 percent in 1990. None of us would be discussing a peace dividend in the 1990s had we not incurred the expenses of a modernized armed services in the early part of the decade. In the end the same fundamental problem remains: America's appetite for government services exceeds the willingness to be taxed for them by about 2 percent of GNP. It has not changed much.

Clearly some want to spend the "peace divided" for the social deficit. But it is time to talk some basic numbers, based on our own Budget Committee calculations and extrapolating Secretary Cheney's $180 billion reduction. Defense will decline from about 5.4 percent of GNP today to 4 percent in 1994.

When he appeared before the Senate Budget Committee a month ago, Lawrence Korb suggested we should be spending about $225 billion in 1995, expressed in 1990 dollars. That is approximately 3.5 or 3.6 percent of GNP. My chairman, Senator Sasser, has suggested we go much further.

I do not know what the number should be. Much like Rudy Penner, I wish we would not approach it in terms of percentages and real rates of growth. We should approach defense the old-fashioned way as we do other programs: through our policies, our goals, our missions and objectives. And certainly we should not do this unilaterally.

For that reason, if none other, 1991 will be restrained through the Conventional Forces in Europe negotiations and the Strategic Arms Reductions Talks. And those have to be followed by Senate ratification. But whatever the outcome, if you look back over the fifty years of history on budget numbers, only two times in the history of this country have we ever spent below 4 percent of GNP for defense: 1940, not too good a year, and 1948. Possibly—with the long-range economic forecast that will be used, the long-range defense plans that Secretary Cheney is working on, and the demographic changes—the Gramm-Rudman target can be reached in 1993 for defense.

But this scenario would not allow for other nondefense spending increases in the aggregate. If there is to be a peace dividend, it will grow until the outyears. You can see it growing into the outyears on the path that Defense is headed: not 1991, but 1994, 1995. If there is a peace dividend, its best use would go toward deficit reduction.

We should not repeat the mistakes of the 1960s and 1970s and create a new entitlement spending program or any programs predicated upon a discretionary peace dividend. Let me close on social security. Some of my conservative friends are now arguing to use this peace dividend as a way to pay for the adoption of the rollback in the payroll taxes.

Notwithstanding the fact that the math does not work under such a proposal, all the reduction of defense under the current peace dividend would be required to balance the budget in 1993. Notwithstanding that, at least the debate has been joined with a real issue as opposed to the fantasy issue of on-budget, off-budget financing. Whether I agree or disagree with modifications is not important. A number of members coming back to town now are finding out about this and are rushing to it. This issue, along with defense, will clearly dominate the early part of the 1990s fiscal policy debate. I would raise only, first of all, a parochial concern and then a few other issues.

First, I will play the role of that greedy postwar baby-boomer. I would question whether a rollback in the payroll taxes is not the beginning of a rollback in future retirement benefits. When the retirement boom hits, without having made my contribution to the fund, would that be a justification for cutting benefits, particularly when payroll taxes have to be raised significantly to make it truly pay-as-you-go?

If the rollback is adopted, however, you have to do what Congressman Gradison was talking about: look at the next step. Three options are available if this particular proposal is adopted.

First, there would be a major constraint on defense, to totally irresponsible levels, because as this decade begins, the pendulum has clearly swung and there is no major restraint on nondefense spending comparable to what ushered in the 1980s.

Another scenario is to replace the payroll taxes with income and corporate taxes, maybe not the worst outcome of all from an income distributional perspective but in the near term an unlikely outcome with an administration resisting such taxes. And therefore higher deficits and lower national saving would result in the long run.

The third option, not one that I am terribly supportive of, nor is the congressman, is simply the removal of social security and other trust fund pension programs from the unified budget concept. And therefore we would have to set a whole new set of targets for Gramm-Rudman to carry us completely through the decade of the 1990s.

I see problems with all of these, but in the end some combination of the three is likely to dominate the discussion. Let me close with the long-term outlook. No one can truly forecast the decade. There will be three presidential elections and six congressional elections over this period. But as one who has been associated with the budget process since 1974, I wonder whether that process will survive the 1990s. The problems are well documented, and clearly reform is required.

But without defending the process, let me repeat what is said by those of us who work in the trenches: the process carries its own enforcement mechanisms. Problems such as the payment shifts of on-budget or off-budget activities carry, within the existing rules, opportunities to prevent enforcement. Those same people who cry reform are often the first ones to rush to weigh the budget act to make those things take place. I agree with Congressman Gradison, who suggests that not process but leadership is needed.

Rudy Penner mentioned health care. Let me remind everybody once again that beginning in 1993 Medicare is off-budget. We will have another issue to handle with Medicare in 1993. Another growing public policy and fiscal issue deals with the whole situation with the liabilities, both funded and unfunded, contingent on the various credit, insurance, in-extent, government-sponsored agencies. Rudy Penner mentioned that this may become an issue. It is an issue now. Currently these programs represent at least $5 billion in liabilities to the government, not counting the unfunded liabilities of the pension programs. It is not an issue that is yet to come. It is here with us and we need to address it now.

LAWRENCE J. KORB: Bill Hoagland wishes that we could make defense budgets the old-fashioned way, looking at the threat and then deciding what to spend. About ten years ago for an AEI Public Policy Week, Mel Laird and I put together a paper. This was as Reagan was getting ready to take over the White House and said that we need a defense build-up, not a binge. On the same panel were some of the AEI economists, including Herb Stein, who said, "You know your job is to deal with the threat, let us worry about the economy." About a year or so later Herb did come by the Pentagon and tell me that he wished that my boss Secretary Weinberger would stop giving speeches that the defense spending was good for the economy because we went from one extreme to the other.

Now if you are looking at defense in the future, two things should be kept in mind. The Defense Department and the administration are a day late and a dollar short. They will also have to deal with a revolution of rising or declining expectations. If you look at what has happened over the past few years, you see that the Defense Department, in the early part of the second Reagan administration, said that it needed 6 percent real increases.

Congress said, no, the best you can do is 3 percent. Defense asked for 6 percent, did not get it. Then Defense dropped to 3 percent, and even a year ago, when Reagan and Carlucci presented their last budget to Congress, Defense talked about 2 percent annual real increases. This year, from what we know about the numbers, Defense will request a 2 percent decline.

That will be no more effective than the 2 percent increase a year

95

ago. And it is important to keep in mind how dramatically the reference points are changing. Look at Reagan's last budget, the Reagan-Carlucci budget, presented a year ago.

They said that in fiscal year 1991 we would be spending more than $350 billion annually on defense. The numbers that I see coming out of the administration are close to $300 billion. That is a traumatic change in just a year, and we have not seen the bottom yet. When I talk about the revolution of declining expectations, from a political point of view, Cheney's statement about the $180 billion cuts was the worst thing to do.

One congressman called me to say he did not like Cheney when Cheney was in the House because he voted for every defense program. This congressman had a great deal of concern when Cheney became secretary of defense because he was thought of as a hard-liner.

But the congressman changed his mind. And I asked why. He said that Cheney wants to cut $180 billion from the defense budget next year and bring it down to $120 billion. In a speech criticizing Cheney, Les Aspin made the same point: some of his colleagues are talking about $120 billion next year.

The incoming budget will have a 2 percent real decline, but there will be a nominal increase. And people will look at that and say that despite everything the budget is still going up. Where is this $180 billion you promised us? If you say it is coming next year—and if you read the fine print, I said 1992 to 1994—nobody will want to wait that long.

The world is moving too fast, particularly in the international arena. A year ago people were saying the best that the Department of Defense could hope for is zero real growth. Today the best it could hope for is zero nominal, and it will be lucky to get that in the current environment.

Between 1985 and 1990 defense authority dropped a little more than 13 percent; that was because of Gramm-Rudman, or deficit reduction. People are talking about a peace dividend. Compare the Defense projections before Gramm-Rudman was passed. Defense talked about spending just about $2 trillion between fiscal years 1986 and 1990.

Actually defense authority for that period was about $1.4 trillion. So $600 billion was cut from that plan after Gramm-Rudman. To the extent that you were going to spend that $600 billion, there was some sort of a dividend. Where did it go? It went primarily to deficit reduction.

We can talk about gimmicks and numbers, but the fact is that the annual budget deficit is smaller, both in absolute terms and as a percentage of the GNP, than when Gramm-Rudman was passed. Defense has been victimized by the Willy Sutton principle—he robbed banks, you'll remember, because that's where the money is.

People went after Defense not because the threat was declining, but because the money was there, particularly because nobody was willing to raise taxes. Since George Bush has been in office, he has cut the defense program he inherited on three separate occasions. That is quite good in one year.

He cut it February 9, 1989. There was no secretary of defense yet. He said he would freeze the defense for fiscal year 1990 and then make some further reductions for the outyears; that was about a $45 billion cut. In the budget summit with Bush, Cheney, and Congress, they cut another $20 billion. Based upon the numbers that I have seen, the cuts over that five-year program, including Cheney's $180 billion, are about $250 billion, which Cheney has cut, by himself, in the first year.

If an administration that was elected as hard-line on defense is to do that, the Congress controlled by the opposite party, which felt that its candidate was beaten up on the defense issue, may go even further.

I agree with everything said here about focusing on the size of the defense budget. Certainly the size is important, but much more important is what you spend it on. Somehow that seems to get lost. The Bush administration and Secretary Cheney and Congress will confront several problems this year, with whatever number they devise.

First, the program and budget are still way out of balance. When Ronald Reagan left the presidency, he bequeathed to his successor a $400 billion defense program; even when he left, his budget numbers were closer to $300 billion. About $1 trillion worth of weapons systems in the defense pipeline somehow or another needs to be accommodated.

You have to bring those two, program and budget, back into balance. More important, you need a long-term policy that convinces the American people that we need a substantial defense without a demon driving foreign policy or without the evil empire or godless atheism. We need to convince the American people that we have to grow up and play big-power politics, that we are a great nation and there will be great threats to our nation that require military force even without an ideological enemy.

I do not know if this administration, at least in its first term, will be capable of doing this. It started off on the right foot doing a strategic review. Unfortunately, as *Aviation Week and Space Technology* noted, that strategic review turned out to be a nullity. The Defense Department's planning guidance for its budgets has no impact until 1992.

This budget is a tread-water budget. We know we have to do things, but we have not put our act together yet; can you please wait until next year? And even in the best of circumstances international events may be changing so quickly that it is hard to develop a coherent plan. But certainly if it is not done in the strategic review, everything becomes much more difficult.

The third problem is the economic dependence of certain sectors and certain areas of the country on defense. We saw what happened last year when Cheney correctly tried to bring the program and budget together and decided to cancel weapon systems. After all, Congress had been screaming at Weinberger to do this for years: cancel some systems to get program and budget in line. He canceled some, and then the whole question of economic dependence of certain areas of the country, particularly the case of Grumman, on Long Island, won the day.

Many people argue that we do not need an industrial policy, we do not need economic adjustment, and we ought to let the free market operate on its own. The way I read the 1990 budget, we had economic adjustment. We gave Grumman $1.5 billion to buy eighteen planes that the Department of Defense says it does not need.

And as the budget keeps decreasing each year, there will be more and more of those fights. As a result of last year's congressional add ons many people say that we have a military-industrial complex and we will never cut defense. The top line did not change.

That money was not taken from the social security trust fund; it was taken from other defense contractors. To a certain extent, since much of it came from the B-2 program and SDI, Northrop ended up helping to keep Grumman in business.

Let me conclude on a couple of optimistic notes. Although defense will go down, it should not be reduced quite as rapidly as some people think; we have to live in the real world, which is not a completely rational world, but is a political world. One good thing is that the armed forces are in relatively good shape.

In the 1980s we had a war-time buildup without a war. Defense spending in the first Reagan administration increased more rapidly than during the Vietnam War. We have lot of good equipment, a lot of good men and materiel. We can weather the storm for a few years if we have to.

These cuts are a ratification of the decreased military threat from the Soviet Union. They also allow more room in the defense budget. Whatever we do, we need to plan for the long haul. We need to do it gradually. I would be much more comfortable reducing the budget 5 percent a year over ten years, than reducing it 1 percent, 1 percent, and then 10 or 12 percent in the succeeding years.

In terms of the objective situation there are some optimistic things but also some things that concern me. First, the administration made a terrible mistake this year in deciding on the outlay number for defense before it decided on the authority number. The outlay number is meaningless in defense. It is primarily a product of decisions made in the past. If we want to save money in defense, and we want a peace dividend, we should begin cutting the spending authority. After the battle between Cheney and Darman, the outlay number of about $286 billion resulted.

That order of decisions results in dumb decisions in authority. The relationship of outlays to authority should be about four to one. For every dollar in outlays, there should be four in authority, to do it right. We have lost several billion dollars in outlays. Nobody wants to give up $28 billion in authority, so those programs were picked that minimize the impact on authority. That's okay for the short run, but it causes great long-term damage. Given how Congress handled the 1990 budget, unless the administration very quickly can come up with a strategic plan in that budget document, we will end up as we did last year.

If they were giving awards for congressional bravery or political bravery, they should give one to Les Aspin for what he tried to do last year. When Cheney came up with his budget, Aspin said that his plan was not great but at least he had one, a better one than what they had on the Hill, so he called for a straight up-and-down vote on the plan.

The vote was an 18–18 tie in committee; he lost. Everything went up for grabs. To the extent that Cheney had a plan, it emphasized strategic areas and began cutting back conventional programs. Congress funded the conventional programs by cutting back some of the strategic programs. We ended up with the worst of all possible worlds.

We have eighteen F-14Ds, which the secretary of defense says we do not need. Congress kept alive the V-22, which the secretary says we do not need. We bought thirty-six more helicopters for the army, which we do not need. The B-2 program was stretched out, driving up the unit cost. Whatever number of B-2s we build, the unit cost will be about a billion dollars. And we have SDI, which is neither fish nor fowl. It is too big to be a research program, too small to be any type of deployment program.

JOHN H. MAKIN: Although all the other speakers have demurely and appropriately suggested that they do not want to concentrate on the issue of the payroll tax raised by Senator Moynihan, I am throwing caution to the wind and will focus on that issue because it may be a watershed issue. I also claim some legitimacy here. More than a year ago I wrote a column for the *Washington Times* entitled "The Social Security Surplus Scam," a title that was shamelessly stolen last week by George Will and the *Washington Post*. At the end of my effort I said that I keep wondering when some politician will have the sense to realize that proposing a lower payroll tax would garner two votes from workers for every vote lost from retirees.

And I wonder if even Senator Moynihan reads the *Washington Times*. Here we have a remarkable development. A politician proposes a tax cut, and it is a payroll tax cut, a cut in a tax that is the major tax for 75 percent of taxpayers. That is for 75 percent of taxpayers, the payroll tax is greater than the income tax.

It sounds like a dog-bites-man story. Politician proposes tax cut for most taxpayers. That is what Senator Moynihan is doing. The only remarkable thing is that it took this long to do. Some of the reasons are perhaps political. In 1981 and 1985 Republicans learned that to mention the term "social security" could lead to an election loss.

And although many have been sorely tempted to raise this issue, they have been nervous about it. Even the White House seems nervous about discussing the payroll tax issue. I have a satisfying picture of the Congress and the White House tossing this hot potato among them.

Along with many others, I always suggested that the payroll tax is highly regressive and this was a good reason for eliminating it. The tax rate is levied on the first $50,000 of income now, $54,000 next year. And so the tax rate for lower-income taxpayers is higher than for high-income taxpayers, however the degree of regressivity of the payroll tax has come down sharply.

In 1971 the ceiling, that is, the top income on which the tax was assessed, was about three-quarters of median family income. That is a very regressive tax. Next year the ceiling of $54,300 is 140 percent of median family income. And so it happens that 80 percent of all taxpayers now pay the full rate, which is much higher than in the 1970s.

Taxpayers who are less passive and more chatty about their tax burden are beginning to notice that the payroll tax is a significant burden. I do not know whether this entered into Senator Moynihan's decision to raise the issue, but the discussion will be much more active.

This is no longer a tax that is 1 percent or 3 percent or 4 percent; it is a 15 percent tax on 80 percent of taxpayers, 15 percent of family income—a significant chunk. And so this will be a major issue.

I am often interviewed, when people talk about social security, as a nut who wants to get rid of the system. Most people who interview me do not know what FICA is. And I have concluded over the past year that when people do figure out what FICA is (the Federal Insurance Contributions Act), they will be awfully angry. If you calculate it, FICA, or the payroll tax on your little pay slip, is 7 percent of your gross income.

What most people do not realize, as Gene Steuerle pointed out, is that the tax is really 15 percent. It is really twice what you think you are paying. To understand that, think of a simple example. If I hire you to work for me, I have to pay you your wages, plus 15 percent of that amount to the IRS. You have to earn a marginal product that is worth something that includes your payroll tax. If the payroll tax were eliminated and you were still earning your marginal product, you would have a 15 percent increase in your take-home pay. That is a big chunk. It underscores the notion that Senator Moynihan's proposal will be actively discussed.

Congressman Gradison suggested an interesting question about Senator Moynihan's proposal. If you cut the payroll tax, do you propose an increase in the income tax, or do you propose a cut in social security benefits, or do you propose a cut in some other program? That has been left unspecified.

One of the interesting things to consider here is the budgetary effect and the effect on national saving. The budgetary effect is certainly not a major economic issue, although it may be a major political issue. But the defense "peace dividend" does go some of the way toward effective use of a reduction in the payroll tax.

Yesterday I calculated the dynamics of the deficit if we froze defense at $291 billion, a typical version of the defense dividend, and then eliminated the social security surplus from budgetary calculations. In other words we combined the two. We cut the payroll tax, put social security on a pay-as-you-go basis, and then threw in the defense dividend.

The deficit in 1991 would be about 3.3 percent of GNP, which is what it was in 1988, when the sky was decidedly not falling. In 1994 it would be 2.5 percent of GNP, which is what it will be in fiscal 1990, again when the sky is not falling. The notion that some budget dynamics are going to drive taxes back up is hard to entertain if you look at the numbers.

Now Senator Moynihan makes a great deal of the need for higher national saving and suggests that reducing the payroll tax means getting back onto a budget-balance path. That means an increase in some other taxes. We need to get to a point where we are retiring privately held debt.

Senator Moynihan suggests, in his Dear Colleague letter, that this is tantamount to increasing national saving. That is simply incorrect. If you doubt me, look at the British experience. The British in 1987 amid great self-congratulation moved to a budget surplus and began to retire privately-held government debt. At the same time the private saving rate plummeted virtually to zero. The experience shows that if you eliminate the budget deficit, indeed you do not necessarily eliminate the external deficit because, lo and behold, last year the British external deficit was 4 percent of GNP, which is higher than ours ever reached. Ours peaked at 3.7 percent of GNP in 1987.

The notion that we somehow deal with the national saving problem by treating social security in an actuarial sense or taking social security off budget is one that I do not understand. I look forward to Senator Moynihan's explanation of that point.

It would be important in cutting the payroll tax. It is a great opportunity to remove the disincentives to private saving that are currently in the tax system. By this I mean not an expanded IRA plan or some such approach as the president's proposed saving account, but what economists call marginal incentives to save more. The best way was in the Treasury's original tax reform proposal: allow savers to keep more of each of the interest dollars they earn. Do not tax all of interest income and do not allow full deductibility of interest expense; that is, do not allow people to deduct the inflation portion of interest expense.

The tax code now encourages spending financed by borrowing. If we remove that bias and then discourage borrowing and encourage saving, we will get more saving. It is fashionable to say that the formal economics literature does not support that point. It is controversial. I have worked intensely on that over the past year. My recently published article in the *Review of Economics and Statistics* suggests that personal saving does respond to interest rates in a way that allows us to replace forced saving through the social security system with an increase in personal saving.

The payroll tax and social security are the major issues in fiscal policy over the next few years. We should totally eliminate the payroll tax. We should turn social security into a system that is a safety net, whereby no individual over age sixty-five has an income below the poverty line, simply by virtue of using a negative-income tax.

If your income is below the poverty line, your income is restored to that level by a check from the government. The transition should not be made quickly but over fifteen years so that anybody currently aged fifty or more will proceed under the current system.

But it is time to tell people, particularly the baby-boomers, that we are not prepared to have payroll taxes sufficient to finance their retirement levels through social security. To baby-boomers we should say that in fifteen or twenty years the social security system is going back to a safety net system. You will have an increase in take-home pay on the order of 10 percent. If you want to live better than the safety net level when you retire, you should save more. We would find with the right removal of disincentives from the tax system, removal of saving disincentives, that people would save more.

We would find that a paternal approach to retirement income, like the current system, is not necessary. It says to most Americans that they are too stupid to provide for their retirement, so we will expropriate 12 percent of their income, and 3 percent for Medicare, to force them to do so. We will give it back after they are sixty-five, but we may tax some of it and we may actually make them wait until they are age sixty-seven.

As people understand that system, they will decide that it is not very attractive. Whatever the outcome, I want to thank Senator Moynihan for increasing the attention to this important issue. I look forward to a lively debate over the coming year.

NORMAN J. ORNSTEIN: Our discussion certainly raises enormous doubts about whether we can ever have a fiscal policy that hangs together and that is made with the whole in mind if what we mean by that is a coherent, interrelated set of policies toward taxing, spending, deficit, and debt management.

The social security issue is one example of what we could call the inadvertent fiscal policy that has dominated the last decade or more. We made a series of decisions—in 1981 with tax cuts, in 1983 with the social security reforms, in 1986 with tax reform—that had a major affect of dramatically altering the tax base for the overwhelming majority of people in this country.

We moved from a heavy reliance on the income tax to a heavy reliance on the payroll tax. In 1981, if we had the foresight, we could have said to policy makers, "In the next six to seven years you will tilt the tax system so that 75 percent of the people in this country will have a much heavier burden with the regressive social security tax than with the progressive income tax, and you will greatly alter the income tax to make it much less progressive." And they all would have said that we were crazy, that they would never do a thing like that.

They did not do it explicitly; they did it with a series of separate decisions, many of them made with regard to a narrower goal, sometimes short-term, sometimes not so short-term. And we see now with the debate on social security a great tension has developed. Some tension developed over the simple coherence and nature of the social security system without regard to the deficit issue or the broader budget issue. Some tension comes as we are forced to consider the system in the context of the larger budget issue.

I would address Senator Moynihan's motives. This man was a major architect of the social security reforms in 1983 and is thinking now more specifically and directly with a great deal of frustration about what has become of those reforms. He has tried over the past two years to get people to think about the system and the theory behind those reforms: we would build up large surpluses, with workers of the baby-boom and succeeding generations paying in money, in effect, that would then go toward their own retirement, for the first time in the history of this program.

What was originally sold to the American people as a retirement plan would become that. Senator Moynihan has seen that theory fall apart and has tried to raise warning flags without much success beyond an occasional editorial here or there. He now has found a way to force people to think about this. It is an interesting comment on the nature of debate on policy in this system and on what it takes to rivet attention.

We think about the system on two levels. On one level, if we think of the social security system separate from fiscal policy and the budget in this country, what do we say to workers today in terms of the compact that they have made?

In a short while we will get to the next level of debate on that subject, namely, saying to people of my generation and to the next younger generation, middle-aged people and those below, that you have a couple of choices. This is the choice that Senator Moynihan is giving you. We can cut your payroll taxes now from what they have been and what they would otherwise be, but then we will have to confront what your retirement will be in fifteen, twenty, twenty-five, or thirty years.

And that means saying, How about a bargain? We will extend the retirement age well beyond what it is now and what it is projected, in return for getting money now. If we talk about it in those terms, most workers, at age forty, would think twenty-five years ahead. They would have an extra $1,000 or $2,000 a year in pocket today. Instead of being able to retire at age sixty-two, with 80 percent of the full benefits of social security and retire at age sixty-five with full benefits, they would retire at sixty-nine or seventy. Maybe they would have an early retirement at sixty-five, but for 50 percent of the benefits. Or we can try to keep in place the system where we pay these high payroll taxes, but we cannot guarantee a thing.

My guess is, if that is the choice, most people know what to take. And if we thought of this in social security terms alone, as Senator Moynihan is trying to get us to confront it, we would move away from the theory that we have built up a big surplus. His theory would lead to this particular reform: we can keep the benefit level high and maybe even raise the level by paying out the surplus when the work force changes and think in terms of current taxes and future benefits at another level.

But we cannot do that alone. Fiscal policy will begin to intercede. We have to talk in terms of what it means if we cut the tax now and what it will do to deficits now and what it will do to fiscal policy now. We will see the inadvertent policies of the past come together, and we will have to confront them more directly.

Many Democrats will see the political appeal of a tax cut now for the overwhelming mass of workers. John Makin's original statement of a year ago with two workers for every retiree is not quite accurate in this sense. We are probably not talking about changing benefits for current retirees. We are talking about people paying in now for their own benefits down the road.

We will not see much grumbling from retirees if we cut payroll taxes now as long as we do not cut benefits now. And that will not enter the discussion. Democrats will see that but will not propose a compensating additional tax, even if it is a fairer tax with which to tilt the system.

Rather they will talk much more in terms that do not meet the arithmetic of using the peace dividend to pay for social security tax cuts. And they will also talk at another level: President Bush has had the luxury of selling the American people on the notion that we do not need to pay a price now for deficits that we have had because we have been using the social security fund illegitimately and illicitly to cushion that blow. We will take away that fiction, and now it is up to Bush to decide what we do about deficits. We see already from some signs of incipient panic in Republican ranks, of fear that this will happen. There is an attempt to get on the bandwagon early with a proposal instead of reacting defensively and saying, do not take away this fiction. But nobody is coming forward with the other side. It will be a long time before we see anybody coming forward with the other side.

I would make one other point more strongly than John Makin

would on the issue of social security. We have moved from a system that relied on the progressive income tax to one that relies on the regressive social security tax. Now we are talking about cuts in social security, across-the-board cuts.

I would be surprised if we did not begin to see some attention paid to the structure of the social security tax. Whether we cut it or not, this is a heavy burden, an extraordinarily heavy burden on most workers. I would be surprised if we did not start talking about restructuring that burden. Exempting the first few thousand dollars of income from the payroll tax, for example, would be a far more effective way of giving a wage increase to lower-income people than raising the minimum wage.

And then we could alter the tax structure to make it more progressive. I am not sure this would work in economics terms, but we will have to discuss it because it is the next logical step as we talk about the way in which we have shifted our tax burdens without perhaps thinking about it. But we will start to think about it more.

Finally, we have seen at least one aspect of the 1990s clearly. The issues of social security, health costs, defense, and defense cuts will dominate the 1990s as they began to dominate the 1980s. There is no way around some of the difficult choices that we will face in dealing with those issues.

And none of them promise the kinds of short-term savings for which politicians and the rest of us would hope. Mostly they require some short-term pain to get to long-term savings. That is not easy to swallow in the political process. It assures that the issues will be around perhaps in substantially the same form toward the end of this decade as now.

5

The Decade of the Nineties— America's Golden Age?

Jack F. Kemp

It is hard to believe that only a few short years ago conventional wisdom in economic circles held that the Reagan-Bush economic policy would sink the economy—that tax reductions, budgetary restraint, and the revitalization of free entrepreneurial markets would cause skyrocketing interest rates and plunge the nation into permanent recession.

By the close of the decade of the 1980s this doomsaying was totally discredited not only by American history, but by world history as well. Far from declining in influence, America and the ideals of democracy, freedom, and entrepreneurial capitalism have proven to be a beacon of hope to the peoples of Eastern Europe, Asia, and Africa, who are striving to rebuild their nations following decades of Communist oppression.

The economic lesson of the past decade is that free enterprise and free markets work; government–directed economies do not. For those who, before 1989, still could not see the failures of central planning, the abrupt collapse of the Socialist economies of Eastern Europe has provided an incontestable demonstration of that reality.

No one has expressed it more eloquently than the Czech playwright, Vaclav Havel, now the first post-Communist president of Czechoslovakia. Havel said that socialism "made talented people who were capable of managing their own affairs and making an enterprising living in their own country into cogs in some kind of monstrous, ramshackle machine that can do nothing more than wear itself down along with all the cogs in it."[1]

Economic Achievements and Economic Bogeymen in the 1980s

Democratic victories are becoming almost commonplace, but it is awesome to reflect that if Reagan and Bush had not engineered one of the greatest economic recoveries in American history during the

1980s these great revolutions abroad might not have occurred at all. If the stagflation, despair, and self-doubt of the 1970s had continued, would the world be rushing to embrace the American model?

In the face of success some intellectual and political circles have found it necessary to revise the conventional wisdom. They will insist that the Reagan-Bush policy prescriptions were wrong, but now they charge that those policies led to enormous, dangerous budgetary and trade deficits.

These economists have been tirelessly anticipating a Great Debacle. After the 1987 stock market crash John Kenneth Galbraith wrote, "This debacle marks the last chapter of Reaganomics,"[2] Hobart Rowen of the *Washington Post* said, "The joyride is over,"[3] and Anthony Lewis of the *New York Times* wrote, "The Age of Reagan is over now, no matter what happens."[4]

I am in the company today of fiscal, budgetary, and economic experts. But even as a layman, I cannot fail to notice a large gap between such economic commentary and reality.

The 1980s saw interest rates slashed by more than half and inflation cut by more than two-thirds. We continue to generate and enjoy our nation's longest peacetime expansion. Since it began in December 1982, this expansion has created nearly 20 million new jobs—more than the number created in Europe and Japan combined. Real after-tax personal income has grown by 28.5 percent since 1982.[5] And as for the "horrendous" deficit, it has fallen from 6.1 percent of the gross national product to 3 percent.

In fact, in an article entitled, "The End of Economics," a *Washington Post* deputy editor explores the likelihood that we have seen the end of the traditional business cycle.[6] Is it really possible that America's era of prosperity could continue forever? I think it might be. There is nothing historically inevitable about recession; recession and inflation result from bad government policies. Expansions do not die of old age; they are killed by bad policies. How many recessions has Japan had in the past twenty years?

The apparently undamaged credibility of the doomsayers, despite all their erroneous predictions, caused one newspaper editor to write that "They might have called Reagan the Teflon president, but there apparently was plenty of the stuff to go around."[7]

Let me put to rest one myth: supply side economics was not predicated on the Laffer curve; it was predicated on the classical, liberal, capitalistic idea that people cannot consume unless someone produces. Jean-Baptiste Say, while not perfect in his economics, did have something to say to the world when he made that point. Before one consumes, one must produce.

Challenges in the 1990s

I believe the greatest promise for the 1990s is not just global democracy, but global democratic entrepreneurial capitalism. And our challenge is, What can we do to provide that model of democratic capitalism for Eastern Europe, Asia, Latin America, Africa—including South Africa—and third world countries who have to deal with their problems of housing, jobs, and poverty? Is our model good enough?

The economic challenges we face today are vastly different from those of the 1980s. The central issue of the past decade was solving stagflation. In my view, the major issue of the 1990s will be spreading the revolution of freedom abroad and strengthening the economic expansion in our own nation's ghettos and barrios.

The next frontier of U.S. economic and fiscal policy is to demonstrate that free markets and free enterprise are the greatest weapons against poverty ever devised in the history of mankind. If the world is to continue seeing the United States as the model to follow, we must reject the idea that poverty is permanent for some in our nation. We must wage a new war on poverty, one that puts destitution and need back on the path of decline where they have been for most of our history.

President Bush believes this. For the first time in decades a Republican administration has introduced a far-reaching new anti-poverty program: HOPE, Homeownership and Opportunity for People Everywhere. HOPE will empower poor people with greater control over their lives and communities, strengthen the link between effort and reward, and create pride of ownership and self-discipline. President Bush's HOPE initiative is the first salvo of a new war on poverty in the 1990s.

We want to alter the rewards and incentives in the inner city. We are trying to alter the behavior of the inner city economy and people in these pockets of poverty. The current incentives are perverse, totally at odds with everything we have been taught in our society and by our parents. We have to show people that the reward for staying in school, studying, qualifying, and moving up is greater than the reward for leaving and going out on the streets; the reward for keeping a family together is greater than the reward for breaking it up; the reward for taking a job if you're on welfare and unemployment is greater than the reward for staying on welfare and unemployment.

In Washington, D.C., if a woman on welfare who has two or three children takes a job with Oliver Carr or McDonald's, her income goes down because the government discontinues her welfare payments and taxes her income. She would need to earn $15,000 of nominal, taxable income in the private sector to match her previous nontaxable transfer payment income of $9,000 or $10,000. This is a perverse incentive. Not only is it at odds with everything that makes our economy work; it is at odds with how we should treat people, who are a resource for our country.

There are entrepreneurs in the ghettos and barrios who are just waiting to burst forth with ideas if we can reduce the barriers and impediments that prevent them from doing what they would like to do—if the economy were as open to entrepreneurship in the inner city as it is generally throughout our country today.

Fiscal Policy Issues

Obviously, a healthy, vigorous national economy must be the foundation for any war on poverty. President Bush's plan to cut the capital gains tax could propel a new wave of prosperity that will sweep into every last pocket of poverty remaining in America.

President Bush has roundly condemned the demogogic claim that only the rich realize the benefit of capital gains tax reductions. Average- and low-income Americans have accrued trillions of dollars in capital gains in their homes, stocks, and mutual funds and, indirectly, through pensions and insurance funds. Moreover, it is the poor and middle-income earners who need greater access to new seed capital in order to become the next generation of entrepreneurs and risk takers.

The capital gains tax reduction will help unlock capital from existing enterprises and lower-risk investments so that it can be used for the new small businesses, new entrepreneurship, and new risk taking that are essential to a thriving economy of opportunity.

The Treasury Department estimates that a reduction of the tax rate to 15 percent would boost asset sales by 91 percent in fiscal year 1991, to a total of $349 billion. These additional sales would give the enterprising poor and small-business owners an enormous boost in gaining access to new seed capital for business start-ups or expansion.

A lower capital gains tax rate also increases the willingness of investors to take a chance on small, precarious firms whose long-term success is far from guaranteed—precisely the type of firms that are most likely to originate in depressed communities.

Moreover, entrepreneurs and small-business owners are more likely to start businesses if they expect to receive 100 percent of the rewards of their efforts. In fast-growing small enterprises, capital gains are far more significant to the owner–manager than in large businesses where managers are heavily compensated through salaries and bonuses. Thus the capital gains tax reduction is a critical component of a strategy to revitalize capitalism in the inner city. And as we reduce the capital gains tax rate for the nation, we should abolish it entirely in enterprise zones throughout the nation where poverty, despair, and joblessness are rampant.

Some have talked about a "peace dividend" as the need for military force seems to have receded, with Eastern Europe moving toward democratic freedom and the Soviet Union experimenting with reform. President Bush has rightly cautioned that it is premature to think of radical reductions in the U.S. defense budget. But I do not believe it is too early to think of a "growth dividend" in the 1990s. If expansion continues and interest rates return to more normal levels, the decade of the 1990s may be a period of budget balance or even surplus. In my view a growth dividend will raise exciting possibilities for dramatic tax reduction and prudent new initiatives such as the HOPE program to fight poverty, create jobs, and expand equal opportunity.

I am looking forward to the debate on social security that Senator Moynihan has started with his suggestion for large cuts in social security taxes. That is not the only tax cut worth considering. Many conservatives have recommended increases in the personal exemption to help offset the antifamily bias of the tax code. The exemption would need to be at least doubled to compensate for the effects of inflation since 1948. The real debate in our country concerns not which taxes to raise but which taxes to cut in order to promote economic growth and achieve other social goals.

Conclusion

We are told by the great conservative writer Richard Weaver that ideas have consequences.[8] What a spectacular day it was when in October 1989 the workers in the Soviet Union celebrated the glorious revolution of 1917 by carrying a sign that read, "Workers of the world, we're sorry."

Can we learn from our history and avoid that kind of mistake again? Hegel said the only thing people learn from history is that nobody learns anything from history. I don't believe that, I think people do learn from history.

The decade of the 1990s should be one of the most exciting times in world history. Communism is a dying ideology. The cold war is changing and subsiding. It should be a decade of infinite possibilities, a golden age for freedom and democracy, with unprecedented expansion of America's prosperity and influence. After a century on the defensive, the forces of freedom abroad and progress against poverty at home are linked in one great cause for good.

111

Notes

INTRODUCTION, *David Zlowe*

1. J. C. Polanyi. "Dangers of Nuclear War." *Bulletin of Atomic Scientists*, vol. 36 (January 1980), pp. 6–10.
2. George L. Perry. "Editor's Summary." *Brookings Papers on Economic Activity*, vol. 1 (Brookings Institution, 1980), p. 7.
3. *New York Times*, January 29, 1980.
4. Gottfried Haberler. "The President's Economic Malaise." *Contemporary Economic Problems* (American Enterprise Institute, 1979), p. 261.
5. "Can We Govern? The Traumas of the 70s—the Challenges of the 80s." *National Journal*, vol. 3 (Government Research Corporations), p. 81.
6. Michael Barone, Grant Ujifusa, and Douglas Matthews. Introduction to *The Almanac of American Politics* (New York: E. P. Dutton, 1979), p. xi.

CHAPTER 1: DEBT AND DEFICITS, *Rudiger Dornbusch and James M. Poterba*

1. See Herbert Stein, *The Fiscal Revolution in America* (Chicago: University of Chicago Press, 1969), for a definitive history of the debate on debts and deficits.
2. E. H. Young, *The System of National Finance* (London: Smith, Elder, 1915).
3. Robert J. Barro, "The Behavior of United States Deficits," in Robert J. Gordon, ed., *The American Business Cycle: Continuity and Change* (Chicago: University of Chicago Press, 1986), pp. 361–87.
4. A lengthier discussion of deficit measurement issues may be found in Robert Eisner, *How Real Is the Federal Deficit?* (New York: Free Press, 1986), and Olivier J. Blanchard, "Suggestions for a New Set of Fiscal Indicators," mimeo, MIT Department of Economics, 1989.
5. Alan Auerbach and Laurence Kotlikoff, in *Dynamic Fiscal Policy* (New York: Cambride University Press, 1987), present several examples illustrating how measured deficits can misstate actual intergenerational transfers.
6. A more detailed discussion of alternative accounting treatments for deposit insurance may be found in Michael J. Boskin, Kenneth Cone, and Sule Ozler, "The Federal Budget and Deposit Insurance," Center for Economic Policy Research discussion paper no. 10, Stanford University, 1983.
7. U.S. Office of Management and Budget, *Special Analyses: Budget of the United States Government, Fiscal Year 1989* (Washington, D.C.: Government Printing Office, 1988), p. F-40.
8. Robert Eisner, in "Budget Deficits: Rhetoric and Reality," *Journal of Economic Perspectives*, vol. 3 (1989), pp. 73–94, provides a modern statement of this position.

9. Robert J. Barro, "The Neoclassical Approach to Fiscal Policy," in Robert J. Barro, ed., *Handbook of Modern Business Cycle Theory* (Cambridge: Harvard University Press, 1989).

10. This view of the burden of the debt was developed in detail by Franco Modigliani, "Long Run Implications of Alternative Fiscal Policies and the Burden of the Public Debt," *Economic Journal*, vol. 71 (1961), pp. 730–55, and Peter Diamond, "National Debt in a Neoclassical Growth Model," *American Economic Review*, vol. 55 (1965), pp. 1126–50.

11. The time profile of debt repayments is explored in James M. Poterba and Lawrence H. Summers, "Finite Lifetimes and the Effects of Budget Deficits on National Savings," *Journal of Monetary Economics*, vol. 20 (1987), pp. 369–91.

12. Robert J. Barro, "Are Government Bonds Net Wealth?" *Journal of Political Economy*, vol. 82 (1974), pp. 1095–1117.

13. Evidence on the consumption behavior of low-net-worth households is summarized in Stephen P. Zeldes, "Consumption and Liquidity Constraints: An Empirical Investigation," *Journal of Political Economy*, vol. 97 (April 1989), pp. 305–47. Particularly useful evidence, stemming from anticipated changes in social security benefits, is presented in David Wilcox, "Social Security Benefits, Consumption Expenditures, and the Lifecycle Hypothesis," *Journal of Political Economy*, vol. 97 (April 1989), pp. 288–304. Data on the patterns of income and consumption spending over the lifecycle for various occupations and income groups are presented in Chris Carroll and Lawrence Summers, "The Lifecycle Hypothesis Reconsidered," in D. Bernheim and J. Shoven, eds., *The Economics of Saving* (Chicago: University of Chicago Press, forthcoming).

14. D. Bernheim, "Ricardian Equivalence: An Evaluation of Theory and Evidence," in S. Fischer, ed., *NBER Macroeconomics Annual 1987*, (Cambridge: MIT Press, 1987), pp. 263–303.

15. Jerry A. Hausman, "Individual Discount Rates and the Purchase and Use of Energy-Saving Durables," *Bell Journal of Economics*, vol. 10 (Spring 1979), pp. 33–54.

16. The principal study on this point is B. Douglas Bernheim and Kyle Bagwell, "Is Everything Neutral?" *Journal of Political Economy*, vol. 96 (1988), pp. 308–38.

17. This point on the political economy of deficit finance is due to Edward M. Gramlich, "Budget Deficits and National Saving: Are Politicians Exogenous?" *Journal of Economic Perspectives*, vol. 3 (1989), pp. 23–35.

18. George Iden and John Sturrock, "Deficits and Interest Rates: Theoretical Issues and Empirical Evidence," Staff Working Papers, Congressional Budget Office, Washington, D.C., January 1989.

19. See Martin Feldstein and Charles Horioka, "Domestic Savings and International Capital Flows," *Economic Journal*, vol. 90 (June 1980), pp. 314–29, and for a review of subsequent work, Michael Dooley et al., "International Capital Mobility: What Do Savings-Investment Correlations Tell Us?" *IMF Staff Papers* (September 1987).

20. The apparent sum of 56 rather than 57 for the parenthesized values reflects rounding errors.

21. These issues are explored in much greater detail in David Cutler, James Poterba, Louise Sheiner, and Lawrence Summers, "Aging Population: Opportunity or Challenge?" *Brookings Papers on Economic Activity*, vol. 1 (forthcoming, 1990).

22. One such study is George Hatsopoulos and Stephen Brooks, "The Gap in the Cost of Capital," in Ralph Landau and Dale Jorgenson, eds., *Technology and Economic Policy* (Cambridge: Ballinger, 1986).

23. Steven Venti and David Wise, "IRAs and Saving," in M. Feldstein, ed., *The Effects of Taxation on Capital Accumulation* (Chicago: University of Chicago Press, 1986), suggest that roughly half of the money contributed to IRAs represented reduced consumption or *new saving*. Daniel Feenberg and Jonathan Skinner, "Sources of IRA Saving," in L. Summers, ed., *Tax Policy and the Economy* 3 (1989), pp. 25–46, show that IRA contributors were also net savers through other taxable channels, providing weak evidence against the shifting hypothesis.

24. Calculations based on the median household yield an optimistic view of the efficacy of IRAs, since the median IRA contributor is wealthier, and has a higher income, than the median household.

25. This assumes a payout rate of 50 percent and an effective capital gains tax rate of 14 percent owing to the benefits of tax deferral on accruing gains.

26. Evidence that repurchases and other "forced realizations" in the equity market are associated with higher consumption is presented in George Hatsopoulos, Paul Krugman, and James Poterba, *Overconsumption* (Washington, D.C.: American Business Congress, 1989).

27. Scaling back the cost of living adjustment on various transfer programs by eliminating these adjustments for a single year yields a more equal distribution of burdens than adopting a "CPI minus X%" rule. The latter scheme, in which benefits rise by a fixed percentage less than the overall inflation rate each year, leads to large real benefit reductions for long-term transfer recipients (such as the extreme aged on social security). It is preferable to avoid these burdens by adopting one-time real benefit reductions for all recipients.

CHAPTER 2: TAX POLICY, C. *Eugene Steuerle*

1. This study was conducted between 1988 and 1989 under my direction when I was deputy assistant secretary of the Treasury for tax analysis. It was finally released, with some analyses deleted, in March 1990. See "Financing Health and Long-term Care: Report to the President and to the Congress," Washington, D.C.: Superintendent of Documents, 1990.

2. See Eugene Steuerle and Susan Wiener, "Spending the Peace Dividend: Lessons from History" (Washington, D.C.: Urban Institute, 1990).

3. See Thomas Neubig and David Joulfaien, "The Tax Expenditure Budget before and after the Tax Reform Act of 1986," Office of Tax Analysis Paper 60, (Washington, D.C.: U.S. Department of the Treasury, 1988).

4. I assume here that social security taxes paid by the employer are really paid by the worker. Several authors provide justification for this assumption.

See, for instance, Edgar K. Browning and Jacqueline M. Browning, *Microeconomic Theory and Applications*, 2nd ed. (Boston: Little, Brown, 1986), pp. 511–15.

5. In the case of workers, the economics literature gives mixed results. See Robert H. Haveman, "How Much Have the Reagan Administration's Tax and Spending Policies Increased Work Effort?" in Charles R. Hulten and Isabel V. Sawhill, eds., *The Legacy of Reaganomics* (Washington, D.C.: Urban Institute, 1984). One difficulty is that some decision making may be social, rather than individualistic, in nature. If so, differences among individuals in tax rates will not correlate very closely over a short period with differences in labor market participation. Among the most commonly cited articles on a significant savings response is Michael J. Boskin, "Taxation, Saving, and the Rate of Interest," *Journal of Political Economy*, vol. 86 (1978), pp. S3–S27. These estimates are debated by E. Philip Howrey and Saul H. Hymans, "The Measurement and Determination of Loanable Funds Saving," in Joseph A. Pechman, ed., *What Should Be Taxed: Income or Expenditure?* (Washington, D.C.: Brookings Institution, 1980). For a recent survey of this literature, see A. Lans Bovenberg, "Tax Policy and National Saving in the United States: A Survey," *National Tax Journal*, vol. 42 (June 1989), pp. 123–38.

6. Here is a more technical calculation. The 7.65 percent tax paid by the employer is not subject to tax. Therefore an employee in the 15 percent income tax bracket pays a combined tax rate of $(0.15 + 0.153)/(1 + 0.0765)$ or just over 28 percent. Many individuals and households actually fall into the 28 percent income tax bracket while still having all earnings subject to social security tax. Single persons with about $25,000 to $45,000 in earnings, for instance, are likely to pay a combined marginal tax rate of $(0.28 + 0.153)/(1 + 0.0765)$ or more than 40 percent. At the highest earned-income levels the income tax rate is again 28 percent, but there is no social security tax.

7. Whatever the equity considerations, findings are often inconclusive about actual behavioral responses. See, for instance, Ronald B. Mincy, "Paradoxes in Black Economic Progress: Incomes, Families, and the Underclass" (Washington, D.C.: Urban Institute, 1989).

8. This issue is treated in depth in Eugene Steuerle, "Federal Policy and the Accumulation of Private Debt in the Postwar United States," in John Shoven, ed., *Taxes and Corporate Restructuring* (Washington, D.C.: Brookings Institution, forthcoming).

9. Harvey Galper and Eugene Steuerle, "Tax Incentives for Saving," *Brookings Review*, vol. 2 (Winter 1983), pp. 16–23.

10. See "The New Tax Law," in Philip Cagan, ed., *Deficits, Taxes, and Economic Adjustments* (Washington, D.C.: American Enterprise Institute, 1987).

11. See Eugene Steuerle, *Taxes, Loans, and Inflation* (Washington, D.C.: Brookings Institution, 1985).

12. U.S. Office of Management and Budget, *Budget of the United States Government, Fiscal Year 1990* (Washington, D.C.: Superintendent of Documents, 1990) pp. 3–25. Numbers cited are for a drop in GNP in fiscal 1990, as reflected in changes in revenues and expenditures for the following fiscal year.

CHAPTER 3: FEDERAL SPENDING ISSUES, *Rudolph G. Penner*

1. The baseline used here was estimated before the end of fiscal 1989. It somewhat overestimated the fiscal 1989 deficit.

2. For a brief description of dissenting views, see Rudolph G. Penner, *Dealing with the Budget Deficit* (Washington, D.C.: National Planning Association, 1989), pp. 18–20.

3. Congressional Budget Office, "Defense Budget Overview," Briefing paper for the National Economic Commission, October 1988.

4. *The 1989 Annual Report of the Board of Trustees of the Old Age Survivors and Disability Trust Funds*, Washington, D.C., April 1989.

5. The notch babies were the first to have their benefits lowered by benefit reforms of the late 1970s. Those born slightly earlier got higher benefits because of the way that the transition to the new rules was structured. The illegitimacy of the claim of the notch babies is well documented in Robert J. Myers, Gary Burtless, Suzanne B. Dilk, and James W. Kelly, *The Social Security Notch: A Study* (Washington, D.C.: National Academy of Social Insurance), November 1988.

6. Henry J. Aaron, Barry P. Bosworth, and Gary Burtless, *Can America Afford to Grow Old* (Washington, D.C.: Brookings Institution, 1988), p. 28.

7. The data underlying the discussion of infrastructure investments were obtained from W. David Montgomery, Michael D. Deitch, and Elizabeth A. Pinkston, "Lessons from the Past, Opportunities for the Future: The Changing Role of Public Investment in Economic Growth," Colloquium on the Nation's Infrastructure Policy, Washington, D.C., November 17, 1989.

CHAPTER 5: AMERICA'S GOLDEN AGE, *Jack F. Kemp*

1. Vaclav Havel, "Our Freedom," *Washington Post*, January 3, 1990.

2. "Notable and Quotable," *Wall Street Journal*, December 11, 1989.

3. "Notable and Quotable."

4. "Notable and Quotable."

5. "Current Employment Statistics Survey," U.S. Bureau of Labor Statistics, December, 1989; "Survey of Current Business," U.S. Department of Commerce, table 2.1, September 1989.

6. Jodie T. Allen, "The End of Economics," *Washington Post*, January 7, 1990.

7. "Notable and Quotable."

8. Richard Weaver, *Ideas Have Consequences* (Chicago: University of Chicago Press, 1984).

Index

A NOTE ON THE BOOK

*This book was edited by Cheryl Weissman, Dana Lane, and Ann Petty of
the publications staff of the American Enterprise Institute.
The index was prepared by Shirley Kessel,
and the figures were drawn by Hördur Karlsson.
The text was set in Platino, a typeface designed by the twentieth-century
Swiss designer Hermann Zapf. Coghill Composition Company,
of Richmond, Virginia, set the type, and Edwards Brothers Incorporated,
of Ann Arbor, Michigan, printed and bound the book,
using permanent acid-free paper.*

The AEI Press is the publisher for the American Enterprise Institute for Public
Policy Research, 1150 17th Street, N.W., Washington, D.C. 20036: *Christopher
C. DeMuth*, publisher; Edward Styles, director: *Dana Lane*, editor; *Ann Petty*,
editor; *Cheryl Weissman*, editor; *Susan Moran*, editorial assistant (rights and
permissions). Books published by the AEI Press are distributed by arrangement with the University Press of America, 4720 Boston Way, Lanham, Md.
20706.